Dugald Clerk

The Theory of the gas Engine

Dugald Clerk

The Theory of the gas Engine

ISBN/EAN: 9783743316508

Manufactured in Europe, USA, Canada, Australia, Japa

Cover: Foto ©ninafisch / pixelio.de

Manufactured and distributed by brebook publishing software (www.brebook.com)

Dugald Clerk

The Theory of the gas Engine

IN THE SARGASSO SEA

THOMAS A. JANVIER

IN THE SARGASSO SEA

A Novel

BY

THOMAS A. JANVIER

AUTHOR OF
"THE UNCLE OF AN ANGEL" "THE AZTEC TREASURE-HOUSE"
"STORIES OF OLD NEW SPAIN" ETC.

NEW YORK AND LONDON
HARPER & BROTHERS PUBLISHERS
1898

BY THE SAME AUTHOR.

THE AZTEC TREASURE-HOUSE. A Romance of Contemporaneous Antiquity. Illustrated by FREDERIC REMINGTON. Post 8vo, Cloth, $1 50.

This powerful story may well be ranked among the wonder books. No story-reader should miss it, for it is different from anything he has ever read.—*Christian at Work*, N. Y.

THE UNCLE OF AN ANGEL, and Other Stories. Post 8vo, Cloth, $1 25; Paper, 50 cents.

Janvier stands in the first rank as a writer of short stories, and a new volume coming from him is sure to meet with success. In the present instance it well deserves to, for the stories it contains, from the one which gives it its title to the last between the covers, are among his best.—*Christian at Work*, N. Y.

IN OLD NEW YORK. With 13 Maps and 58 Illustrations. Post 8vo, Cloth, $1 75.

Overflows with all sorts of minute and curious information concerning both the old and the recent town. . . . Mr. Janvier has long been a zealous and sympathetic student of this subject. His text is supplemented with numerous maps and illustrations, instructive and interesting.—*N. Y. Sun.*

NEW YORK AND LONDON:
HARPER & BROTHERS, PUBLISHERS.

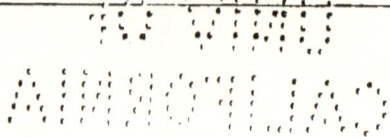

Copyright, 1898, by HARPER & BROTHERS.

All rights reserved.

TO
C. A. J.

CONTENTS

CHAPTER	PAGE
I. I Pay for My Passage to Loango	1
II. How I Boarded the Brig *Golden Hind*	8
III. I Have a Scare, and Get Over It	17
IV. Captain Luke Makes Me an Offer	25
V. I Give Captain Luke My Answer	36
VI. I Tie Up My Broken Head, and Try to Attract Attention	44
VII. I Encounter a Good Doctor and a Violent Gale	52
VIII. The *Hurst Castle* is Done For	59
IX. On the Edge of the Sargasso Sea	66
X. I Take a Cheerful View of a Bad Situation	73
XI. My Good Spirits are Wrung Out of Me	80
XII. I Have a Fever and See Visions	87
XIII. I Hear a Strange Cry in the Night	95
XIV. Of My Meeting with a Murdered Man	103
XV. I Have Some Talk with a Murderer	110
XVI. I Rid Myself of Two Dead Men	119
XVII. How I Walked Myself into a Maze	126
XVIII. I Find the Key to a Sea Mystery	134
XIX. Of a Good Plan that went Wrong with Me	142

CONTENTS

CHAPTER		PAGE
XX.	How I Spent a Night Wearily	150
XXI.	My Thirst is Quenched, and I Find a Compass	157
XXII.	I Get Some Food in Me, and Form a Crazy Plan	164
XXIII.	How I Started on a Journey Due North	171
XXIV.	Of What I Found Aboard a Spanish Galleon	178
XXV.	I Am the Master of a Great Treasure	186
XXVI.	Of a Strange Sight that I Saw in the Night-time	192
XXVII.	I Set Myself to a Heavy Task	199
XXVIII.	How I Rubbed Shoulders with Despair	205
XXIX.	I Get into a Sea Charnel-house	213
XXX.	I Come to the Wall of My Sea-prison	220
XXXI.	How Hope Died Out of My Heart	228
XXXII.	I Fall in with a Fellow-prisoner	236
XXXIII.	I Make a Glad Discovery	243
XXXIV.	I End a Good Job Well, and Get a Set-back	250
XXXV.	I Am Ready for a Fresh Hazard of Fortune	260
XXXVI.	How My Cat Promised Me Good Luck	268
XXXVII.	How My Cat Still Farther Cheered Me	275
XXXVIII.	How I Fought My Way Through the Sargasso Weed	280
XXXIX.	Why My Cat Called Out to Me	286

IN THE SARGASSO SEA

IN THE SARGASSO SEA

I

I PAY FOR MY PASSAGE TO LOANGO

CAPTAIN LUKE CHILTON counted over the five-dollar notes with a greater care than I thought was necessary, considering that there were only ten of them; and cautiously examined each separate one, as though he feared that I might be trying to pay for my passage in bad money. His show of distrust set my back up, and I came near to damning him right out for his impudence—until I reflected that a West Coast trader must pretty well divide his time between cheating people and seeing to it that he isn't cheated, and so held my tongue.

Having satisfied himself that the tale was correct and that the notes were genuine, he brought out from the inside pocket of his long-tailed shore-going coat a big canvas pocket-book, into which he stowed them lengthwise; and from the glimpse I had of it I fancied that until my money got there it was about bare. As he put away the pocket-book, he said, and pleasantly enough:

"You see, Mr. Stetworth, it's this way: fifty dollars is dirt cheap for a cast across from New York to the Coast, and that's a fact; but you say that it's an object with you to get your passage low, and I say that even at that price I can make money out of you. The *Golden Hind* has got to call at Loango, anyhow; there's a spare room in her cabin that'll be empty if you don't fill it; and while you're a big man and look to be rather extra hearty, I reckon you won't eat more'n about twenty dollars' worth of victuals—counting 'em at cost—on the whole run. But the main thing is that I want all the spot cash I can get a-holt of before I start. Fifty dollars' worth of trade laid in now means five hundred dollars for me when I get back here in New York with what I've turned it over for on the Coast. So, you see, if you're suited, I'm suited too. Shake! And now we'll have another drink. This time it's on me."

We shook, and Captain Luke gave me an honest enough grip, just as he had spoken in an honest enough tone. I knew, of course, that in a general way he must be a good deal of a rascal—he couldn't well be a West Coast trader and be anything else; but then his rascality in general didn't matter much so long as his dealings with me were square. He called the waiter and ordered arrack again—it

I PAY FOR MY PASSAGE TO LOANGO

was the most wholesome drink in the world, he said—and we touched glasses, and so brought our deal to an end.

That a cheap passage to Loango was an object to me, as Captain Luke had said, was quite true. It was a very important object. After I got across, of course, and my pay from the palm-oil people began, I would be all right; but until I could touch my salary I had to sail mighty close to the wind. For pretty much all of my capital consisted of my headful of knowledge of the theory and practice of mechanical engineering which had brought me out first of my class at the Stevens Institute—and in that way had got me the offer from the palm-oil people—and because of which I thought that there wasn't anybody quite my equal anywhere as a mechanical engineer. And that was only natural, I suppose, since my passing first had swelled my head a bit, and I was only three-and-twenty, and more or less of a promiscuously green young fool.

As I looked over Captain Luke's shoulder, while we supped our arrack together—out through the window across the rush and bustle of South Street—and saw a trig steamer of the Maracaibo line lying at her dock, I could not but be sorry that my voyage to Africa would be made under sails. But, on the other hand, I comforted myself by thinking that if the *Golden Hind* were half the clipper her captain made her out to be I should not lose much time—taking into account the roundabout way I should have to go if I went under steam. And I comforted myself still more by thinking what a lot of money I had saved by coming on this chance for a cheap cast across; and I blessed my lucky stars for putting into my head the notion of cruising along South Street that October morning and asking every sailor-like man I met if he knew of a craft bound for the West Coast—and especially for having run me up against Captain Luke Chilton before my cruise had lasted an hour.

The captain looked at his glass so sorrowfully when it was empty that I begged him to have it filled again, and he did. But he took down his arrack this time at a single gulp, and then got up briskly and said that he must be off.

"We don't sail till to-morrow afternoon, on the half flood, Mr. Stetworth," he said, "so you'll have lots of time to get your traps aboard if you'll take a boat off from the Battery about noon. I wouldn't come earlier than that, if I were you. Things are bound to be in a mess aboard the brig to-morrow, and the less you have of it the better. We lie well down the anchorage, you know, only a little this side of Robbin's Reef. Your boatmen will know the place, and they'll find the brig for you if you'll tell 'em where to look for her and that she's painted green. Well, so long." And then Captain Luke shook hands with me again, and so was off into the South Street crowd.

I hurried away too. My general outfit was bought and packed; but the things lying around my lodgings had to be got together, and I had to buy a few articles in the way of sea-stock for my voyage in a sailing vessel that I should not have needed had I gone by the regular steam lines. So I got some lunch inside of me, and after that I took a cab—a bit of extravagance that my hurry justified—and bustled about from shop to shop and got what I needed inside of an hour; and then I told the man to drive me to my lodgings up-town.

It was while I was driving up Broadway—the first quiet moment for thinking that had come to me since I had met Captain Luke on South Street, and we had gone into the saloon together to settle about the passage he had offered me—that all of a sudden the thought struck me that perhaps I had made the biggest kind of a fool of myself; and it struck so hard that for a minute or two I fairly was dizzy and faint.

What earthly proof had I, beyond Captain Luke's bare word for it, that there was such a brig as the *Golden Hind?* What proof had I even—beyond the general look of him and his canvas pocket-book —that Captain Luke was a sailor? And what proof had I, supposing that there was such a brig and that he was a sailor, that the two had anything to do with each other? I simply had accepted for truth all that he told me, and on the strength of his mere assertion that he was a ship-master and was about to sail for the West African coast I had paid him my fifty dollars—and had taken by way of receipt for it no more than a clinking of our glasses and a shake of his hand. I said just now that I was only twenty-three years old, and more or less of a promiscuously green young fool. I suppose that I might as well have left that out. There are some things that tell themselves.

For three or four blocks, as I drove along, I was in such a rage with myself that I could not think clearly. Then I began to cool a little, and to hope that I had gone off the handle too suddenly and too far. After all, there were some chances in my favor the other way. Captain Chilton, I remembered, had told me that he was about to sail for West Coast ports before I asked him for a passage; and had mentioned, also, whereabouts on the anchorage the *Golden Hind* was lying. Had he made these statements after he knew what I wanted there would have been some reason for doubting them; but being made on general principles, without knowledge of what I was after, it seemed to me that they very well might be true. And if they were true, why then there was no great cause for my sudden fit of alarm.

I PAY FOR MY PASSAGE TO LOANGO

However, I was so rattled by my fright, and still so uncertain as to how things were coming out for me, that the thought of waiting until the next afternoon to know certainly whether I had or had not been cheated was more than I could bear. The only way that I could see to settle the matter was to go right away down to the anchorage, and so satisfy myself that the *Golden Hind* was a real brig and really was lying there; and it occurred to me that I might kill two birds with one stone, and also have a reason to give for a visit which otherwise might seem unreasonable, if I were to take down my luggage and put it aboard that very afternoon.

II

HOW I BOARDED THE BRIG *GOLDEN HIND*

HAVING come to this conclusion, I acted on it. I kept the cab at the door while I finished my packing with a rush, and then piled my luggage on it and in it—and what with my two trunks, and my kit of fine tools, and all my bundles, this made tight stowing—and then away I went down-town again as fast as the man could drive with such a load.

We got to the Battery in a little more than an hour, and there I transshipped my cargo to a pair-oared boat and started away for the anchorage. The boatmen comforted me a good deal at the outset by saying that they thought they knew just where the *Golden Hind* was lying, as they were pretty sure they had seen her only that morning while going down the harbor with another fare; and before we were much more than past Bedloe's Island —having pulled well over to get out of the channel and the danger of being run down by one of the swarm of passing craft—they made my mind quite easy by actually pointing her out to me. But al-

HOW I BOARDED THE BRIG

most in the same moment I was startled again by one of them saying to me: "I don't believe you've much time to spare, captain. There's a lighter just shoved off from her, and she's gettin' her tops'ls loose. I guess she means to slide out on this tide. That tug seems to be headin' for her now."

The men laid to their oars at this, and it was a good thing—or a bad thing, some people might think—that they did; for had we lost five minutes on our pull down from the Battery I never should have got aboard of the *Golden Hind* at all. As it was, the anchor was a-peak, and the lines of the tug made fast, by the time that we rounded under her counter; and the decks were so full of the bustle of starting that it was only a chance that anybody heard our hail. But somebody did hear it, and a man—it was the mate, as I found out afterwards—came to the side.

"Hold on, captain," one of the boatmen sang out, "here's your passenger!"

"Go to hell!" the mate answered, and turned inboard again.

But just then I caught sight of Captain Chilton, coming aft to stand by the wheel, and called out to him by name. He turned in a hurry—and with a look of being scared, I fancied—but it seemed to me a good half-minute before he answered me. In this time the men had shoved the boat alongside and had made fast to the main-chains; and just then the tug began to puff and snort, and the towline lifted, and the brig slowly began to gather way. I could not understand what they were up to; but the boatmen, who were quick fellows, took the matter into their own hands, and began to pass in my boxes over the gunwale—the brig lying very low in the water—as we moved along. This brought the mate to the side again, with a rattle of curses and orders to stand off. And then Captain Chilton came along himself—having finished whatever he had been doing in the way of thinking—and gave matters a more reasonable turn.

"It's all right, George," he said to the mate. "This gentleman is a friend of mine who's going out with us" (the mate gave him a queer look at that), "and he's got here just in time." And then he turned to me and added: "I'd given you up, Mr. Stetworth, and that's a fact—concluding that the man I sent to your lodgings hadn't found you. We had to sail this afternoon, you see, all in a hurry; and the only thing I could do was to rush a man after you to bring you down. He seems to have overhauled you in time, even if it was a close call—so all's well."

While he was talking the boatmen were passing aboard my boxes and bundles, while the brig went ahead slowly; and when they all were shipped, and I had paid the men, he gave me his hand in a friendly way and helped me up the side.

HOW I BOARDED THE BRIG

What to make of it all I could not tell. Captain Luke told a straight enough story, and the fact that his messenger had not got to me before I started did not prove that he lied. Moreover, he went on to say that if I had not got down to the brig he had meant to leave my fifty dollars with the palm-oil people at Loango, and that sounded square enough too. At any rate, if he were lying to me I had no way of proving it against him, and he was entitled to the benefit of the doubt; and so, when he had finished explaining matters—which was short work, as he had the brig to look after—I did not see my way to refusing his suggestion that we should call it all right and shake hands.

For the next three hours or so—until we were clear of the Hook and had sea-room and the tug had cast us off—I was left to my own devices: except that a couple of men were detailed to carry to my state-room what I needed there, while the rest of my boxes were stowed below. Indeed, nobody had time to spare me a single word—the captain standing by the wheel in charge of the brig, and the two mates having their hands full in driving forward the work of finishing the lading, so that the hatches might be on and things in some sort of order before the crew should be needed to make sail.

The decks everywhere were littered with the stuff put aboard from the lighter that left the brig just before I reached her, and the huddle and confusion showed that the transfer must have been made in a tearing hurry. Many of the boxes gave no hint of what was inside of them; but a good deal of the stuff—as the pigs of lead and cans of powder, the many five-gallon kegs of spirits, the boxes of fixed ammunition, the cases of arms, and so on—evidently was regular West Coast "trade." And all of it was jumbled together just as it had been tumbled aboard.

I was surprised by our starting with the brig in such a mess—until it occurred to me that the captain had no choice in the matter if he wanted to save the tide. Very likely the tide did enter into his calculations; but I was led to believe a little later—and all the more because of his scared look when I hailed him from the boat—that he had run into some tangle on shore that made him want to get away in a hurry before the law-officers should bring him up with a round turn.

What put this notion into my head was a matter that occurred when we were down almost to the Hook, and its conclusion came when we were fairly outside and the tug had cast us off; otherwise my boxes and I assuredly would have gone back on the tug to New York—and I with a flea in my ear, as the saying is, stinging me to more prudence in my dealings with chance-met mariners and their offers of cheap passages on strange craft.

When we were nearly across the lower bay, the

HOW I BOARDED THE BRIG

nose of a steamer showed in the Narrows; and as she swung out from the land I saw that she flew the revenue flag. Captain Luke, standing aft by the wheel, no doubt made her out before I did; for all of a sudden he let drive a volley of curses at the mates to hurry their stowing below of the stuff with which our decks were cluttered. At first I did not associate the appearance of the cutter with this outbreak; but as she came rattling down the bay in our wake I could not but notice his uneasiness as he kept turning to look at her and then turning forward again to swear at the slowness of the men. But she was a long way astern at first, and by the time that she got close up to us we were fairly outside the Hook and the tug had cast us off —which made a delay in the stowing, as the men had to be called away from it to set enough sail to give us steerage way.

Captain Luke barely gave them time to make fast the sheets before he hurried them back to the hatch again; and by that time the cutter had so walked up to us that we had her close aboard. I could see that he fully expected her to hail us; and I could see also that there seemed to be a feeling of uneasiness among the crew, though they went on briskly with their work of getting what remained of the boxes and barrels below. And then, being close under our stern, the cutter quietly shifted her helm to clear us—and so slid past us, without hailing and with scarcely a look at us, and stood on out to sea.

That the captain and all hands so manifestly should dread being overhauled by a government vessel greatly increased my vague doubts as to the kind of company that I had got into; and at the very moment that the cutter passed us these doubts were so nearly resolved into bad certainties that my thoughts shot around from speculation upon Captain Luke's possible perils into consideration of what seemed to be very real perils of my own.

With the cutter close aboard of us, and with the captain and both the mates swearing at them, I suppose that the men at the hatch — who were swinging the things below with a whip—got rattled a little. At any rate, some of them rigged the sling so carelessly that a box fell out from it, and shot down to the main-deck with such a bang that it burst open. It was a small and strongly made box, that from its shape and evident weight I had fancied might have arms in it. But when it split to bits that way—the noise of the crash drawing me to the hatch to see what had happened — its contents proved to be shackles: and the sight of them, and the flash of thought which made me realize what they must be there for, gave me a sudden sick feeling in my inside!

In my hurried reading about the West Coast—

carried on at odd times since my meeting with the palm-oil people—I had learned enough about the trade carried on there to know that slaving still was a part of it; but so small a part that the matter had not much stuck in my mind. But it was a fact then (as it also is a fact now) that the traders who run along the coast—exchanging such stuff as Captain Luke carried for ivory and coffee and hides and whatever offers—do now and then take the chances and run a cargo of slaves from one or another of the lower ports into Mogador: where the Arab dealers pay such prices for live freight in good condition as to make the venture worth the risk that it involves. This traffic is not so barbarous as the old traffic to America used to be—when shippers regularly counted upon the loss of a third or a half of the cargo in transit, and so charged off the death-rate against profit and loss—for the run is a short one, and slaves are so hard to get and so dangerous to deal in nowadays that it is sound business policy to take enough care of them to keep them alive. But I am safe in saying that the men engaged in the Mogador trade are about the worst brutes afloat in our time—not excepting the island traders of the South Pacific—and for an honest man to get afloat in their company opens to him large possibilities of being murdered off-hand, with side chances of sharing in their punishment if he happens to be with them when they are caught.

IN THE SARGASSO SEA

And so it is not to be wondered at that when I saw the shackles come flying out from that broken box, and so realized the sort of men I had for shipmates, that a sweating fright seized me which made my stomach go queer. And then, as I thought how I had tumbled myself into this scrape that the least shred of prudence would have kept me out of, I realized for the second time that day that I was very young and very much of a fool.

III

I HAVE A SCARE, AND GET OVER IT

I WENT to the stern of the brig and looked at the tug, far off and almost out of sight in the dusk, and at the loom of the Highlands, above which shone the light-house lamps—and my heart went down into my boots, and for a while stayed there. For a moment the thought came into my head to cut away the buoy lashed to the rail and to take my chances with it overboard—trusting to being picked up by some passing vessel and so set safe ashore. But the night was closing down fast and a lively sea was running, and I had sense enough to perceive that leaving the brig that way would be about the same as getting out of the frying-pan into the fire.

Fortunately, in a little while I began to get wholesomely angry; which always is a good thing, I think, when a man gets into a tight place—if he don't carry it too far—since it rouses the fighting spirit in him and so helps him to pull through. In reason, I ought to have been angry with myself, for the trouble that I was in was all of my own making; but, beyond giving myself a passing kick or two, all my anger was turned upon Captain Luke for taking advantage of my greenness to land me in such a pickle when his gain from it would be so small. I know now that I did Captain Luke injustice. His subsequent conduct showed that he did not want me aboard with him any more than I wanted to be there. Had I not taken matters into my own hands by boarding the brig in such a desperate hurry—just as I had hurried to close with his offer and to clinch it by paying down my passage-money — he would have gone off without me. And very likely he would have thought that the lesson in worldly wisdom he had given me was only fairly paid for by the fifty dollars which had jumped so easily out of my pocket into his.

But that was not the way I looked at the matter then; and in my heart I cursed Captain Luke up hill and down dale for having, as I fancied, lured me aboard the brig and so into peril of my skin. And my anger was so strong that I went by turns hot and cold with it, and itched to get at Captain Luke with my fists and give him a dressing—which I very well could have done, had we come to fighting, for I was a bigger man than he was and a stronger man, too.

It is rather absurd as I look back at it, considering what a taking I was in and how strong was

I HAVE A SCARE, AND GET OVER IT

my desire just then to punch Captain Luke's head for him, that while I was at the top of my rage he came aft to where I was leaning against the rail and put his hand on my shoulder as friendly as possible and asked me to come down into the cabin to supper. I suppose I had a queer pale look, because of my anger, for he said not to mind if I did feel sickish, but to eat all the same and I would feel better for it; and he really was so cordial and so pleasant that for a moment or two I could not answer him. It was upsetting, when I was so full of fight, to have him come at me in that friendly way; and I must say that I felt rather sheepish, and wondered whether I had not been working myself up over a mare's-nest as I followed him below.

We had the mate to supper with us, at a square table in the middle of the cabin, and at breakfast the next morning we had the second mate; and so it went turn and turn with them at meals—except that they had some sort of dog-watch way about the Saturday night and Sunday morning that always gave the mate his Sunday dinner with the captain, as was the due of his rank.

The mate was a surly brute, and when Captain Chilton said, in quite a formal way, "Mr. Roger Stetworth, let me make you acquainted with Mr. George Hinds," he only grunted and gave me a sort of a nod. He did not have much to say while

IN THE SARGASSO SEA

the supper went on, speaking only when the captain spoke to him, and then shortly; but from time to time he snatched a mighty sharp look at me—that I pretended not to notice, but saw well enough out of the tail of my eye. It was plain enough that he was taking my measure, and I even fancied that he would have been better pleased had I been six inches or so shorter and with less well-made shoulders and arms. When he did speak it was in a growling rumble of a voice, and he swore naturally.

Captain Luke evidently tried to make up for the mate's surliness; and he really was very pleasant indeed—telling me stories about the Coast, and giving me good advice about guarding against sickness there, and showing such an interest in my prospects with the palm-oil people, and in my welfare generally, that I was still more inclined to think that my scare about the shackles was only foolishness from first to last. He seemed to be really pleased when he found that I was not sea-sick, and interested when I told him how well I knew the sea and the management of small craft from my sailing in the waters about Nantucket every summer for so many years; and then we got to talking about the Coast again and about my outfit for it, which he said was a very good one; and he especially commended me—instead of laughing at me, as I was afraid he would—for having

I HAVE A SCARE, AND GET OVER IT

brought along such a lot of quinine. Indeed, the quinine seemed to make a good deal of an impression on him, for he turned to the mate and said: "Do you hear that, George? Mr. Stetworth has with him a whole case of quinine—enough to serve a ship's company through a cruise." And the mate rumbled out, as he got up from the table and started for the deck, that quinine was a damned good thing.

We waited below until the second mate came down, to whom the captain introduced me with his regular formula: "Mr. Roger Stetworth, let me make you acquainted with Mr. Martin Bowers." He was a young fellow, of no more than my own age, and I took a fancy to him at sight—for he not only shook my hand heartily but he looked me squarely in the eyes, and that is a thing I like a man to do. It seemed to me that my being there was a good deal of a puzzle to him; and he also took my measure, but quite frankly—telling me when he had looked me over that if I knew how to steer I'd be a good man to have at the wheel in a gale.

The captain brought out a bottle of his favorite arrack, and he and I had a glass together—in which, as I thought rather hard, Bowers was not given a chance to join us—and then we went on deck and walked up and down for a while, smoking our pipes and talking about the weather and the prospects for the voyage. And it all went so easily and so pleasantly that I couldn't help laughing a little to myself over my scare.

I turned in early, for I was pretty well tired after so lively a day; but when I got into my bunk I could not get to sleep for a long while—although the bunk was a good one and the easy motion of the brig lulled me—for the excitement I was in because my voyage fairly was begun. I slipped through my mind all that had happened to me that day—from my meeting with Captain Luke in the forenoon until there I was, at nine o'clock at night, fairly out at sea; and I was so pleased with the series of lucky chances which had put me on my way so rapidly that my one mischance—my scare about the shackles—seemed utterly absurd.

It was perfectly reasonable, I reflected, for Captain Luke to carry out a lot of shackles simply as "trade." It was pretty dirty "trade," of course, but so was the vile so-called brandy he was carrying out with him; and so, for that matter, were the arms—which pretty certainly would be used in slaving forays up from the Coast. And even supposing the very worst—that Captain Luke meant to ship a cargo of slaves himself and had these irons ready for them—that worst would come after I was out of the brig and done with her; the captain having told me that Loango, which was my landing-place, would be his first port of call. When I was

I HAVE A SCARE, AND GET OVER IT

well quit of the *Golden Hind* she and her crew and her captain, for all that I cared, might all go to the devil together. It was enough for me that I should be well treated on the voyage over; and from the way that the voyage had begun—unless the surly mate and I might have a bit of a flare-up—it looked as though I were going to be very well treated indeed. And so, having come to this comforting conclusion, I let the soft motion of the brig have its way with me and began to snooze.

A little later I was partly aroused by the sound of steps coming down the companion-way; and then by hearing, in the mate's rumble, these words: "I guess you're right, captain. As you had to run for it to-day before you could buy our quinine, it's a damn good thing he did get aboard, after all!"

I was too nearly asleep to pay much attention to this, but in a drowsy way I felt glad that my stock of quinine had removed the mate's objections to me as a passenger; and I concluded that my purchase of such an absurd lot of it—after getting worked up by my reading about the West Coast fevers—had turned out to be a good thing for me in the long-run.

After that the talk went on in the cabin for a good while, but in such low tones that even had I been wide awake I could not have followed it. But I kept dozing off, catching only a word or two now and then; and the only whole sentence I heard was in the mate's rumble again: "Well, if we can't square things, there's always room for one more in the sea."

It all was very dream-like—and fitted into a dream that came later, in the light sleep of early morning, I suppose, in which the mate wore the uniform of a street-car conductor, and I was giving him doses of quinine, and he was asking the passengers in a car full of salt-water to move up and make room for me, and was telling them and me that in a sea-car there always was room for one more.

IV

CAPTAIN LUKE MAKES ME AN OFFER

During the next fortnight or so my life on board the brig was as pleasant as it well could be. On the first day out we got a slant of wind that held by us until it had carried us fairly into the northeast trades—and then away we went on our course, with everything set and drawing steady, and nothing much to do but man the wheel and eat three square meals a day.

And so everybody was in a good humor, from the captain down. Even the mate rumbled what he meant to be a civil word to me now and then; and Bowers and I—being nearly of an age, and each of us with his foot on the first round of the ladder—struck up a friendship that kept us talking away together by the hour at a time: and very frankly, except that he was shy of saying anything about the brig and her doings, and whenever I tried to draw him on that course got flurried a little and held off. But in all other matters he was open; and especially delighted in running on about ships and seafaring—for the man was a born sailor and loved his profession with all his heart.

It was in one of these talks with Bowers that I got my first knowledge of the Sargasso Sea—about which I shortly was to know a great deal more than he did: that old sea-wonder which puzzled and scared Columbus when he coasted it on his way to discover America; and which continued to puzzle all mariners until modern nautical science revealed its cause—yet still left it a good deal of a mystery—almost in our own times.

The subject came up one day while we were crossing the Gulf Stream, and the sea all around us was pretty well covered with patches of yellow weed—having much the look of mustard-plasters—amidst which a bit of a barnacled spar bobbed along slowly near us, and not far off a new pine plank. The yellow stuff, Bowers said, was gulf-weed, brought up from the Gulf of Mexico where the Stream had its beginning; and that, thick though it was around us, this was nothing to the thickness of it in the part of the ocean where the Stream (so he put it, not knowing any better) had its end. And to that same place, he added, the Stream carried all that was caught in its current—like the spar and the plank floating near us—so that the sea was covered with a thick tangle of the weed in which was held fast fragments of wreckage, and stuff washed overboard, and logs adrift

CAPTAIN LUKE MAKES ME AN OFFER

from far-off southern shores, until in its central part the mass was so dense that no ship could sail through it, nor could a steamer traverse it because of the fouling of her screw. And this sort of floating island—which lay in a general way between the Bermudas and the Canaries—covered an area of ocean, he said, half as big as the area of the United States; and to clear it ships had to make a wide detour—for even in its thin outward edges a vessel's way was a good deal retarded and a steamer's wheel would foul sometimes, and there was danger always of collision with derelicts drifting in from the open sea to become a part of the central mass. Our own course, he further said, would be changed because of it; but we would be for a while upon what might be called its coast, and so I would have a chance to see for myself something of its look as we sailed along.

As I know now, Bowers over-estimated the size of this strange island of sea-waifs and sea-weed by nearly one-half; and he was partly wrong as to the making of it: for the Sargasso Sea is not where any current ends, but lies in that currentless region of the ocean that is found to the east of the main Gulf Stream and to the south of the branch which sweeps across the North Atlantic to the Azores; and its floating stuff is matter cast off from the Gulf Stream's edge into the bordering still water —as a river eddies into its pools twigs and dead leaves and such-like small flotsam—and there is compacted by capillary attraction and by the slow strong pressure of the winds.

On the whole, though, Bowers was not very much off in his description—which somehow took a queer deep hold upon me, and especially set me to wondering what strange old waifs and strays of the ocean might not be found in the thick of that tangle if only there were some way of pushing into it and reaching the hidden depths that no man ever yet had seen. But when I put this view of the matter to him I did not get much sympathy. He was a practical young man, without a stitch of romance in his whole make-up, and he only laughed at my suggestion and said that anybody who tried to push into that mess just for the sake of seeing some barnacle-covered logs, or perhaps a rotting hulk or two, would be a good deal of a fool. And so I did not press my fancy on him, and our talks went on about more commonplace things.

It was with Captain Luke that I had most to do, and before long I got to have a very friendly feeling for him because of the trouble that he took to make me comfortable and to help me pass the time. The first day out, seeing that I was interested when he took the sun, he turned the sextant over to me and showed me how to take an observation; and then how to work it out and fix the brig's position on the chart—and was a good deal surprised by my quickness in understanding his explanations (for I suppose that to him, with his rule-of-thumb knowledge of mathematics, the matter seemed complex), and still more surprised when he found, presently, that I really understood the underlying principle of this simple bit of seamanship far better than he did himself. He said that I knew more than most of the captains afloat and that I ought to be a sailor; which he meant, no doubt, to be the greatest compliment that he could pay me. After that I took the sights and worked them with him daily; and as I several times corrected his calculations—for even simple addition and subtraction were more than he could manage with certainty—he became so impressed by my knowledge as to treat me with an odd show of respect.

But in practical matters—knowledge of men and things, and of the many places about the world which he had seen, and of the management of a ship in all weathers—he was one of the best-informed men that ever I came across: being naturally of a hard-headed make, with great acuteness of observation, and with quick and sound reasoning powers. I found his talk always worth listening to; and I liked nothing better than to sit beside him, or to walk the deck with him, while we smoked our pipes together and he told me in his shrewd way about one queer thing and another which he had come upon in various parts of the world—for he had followed the sea from the time that he was a boy, and there did not seem to be a bit of coast country nor any part of all the oceans which he did not know well.

Unlike Bowers, he was very free in talking about the trade that he carried on in the brig upon the African coast, and quite astonished me by his showing of the profits that he made; and he generally ended his discourses on this head by laughingly contrasting the amount of money that even Bowers got every year—the mates being allowed an interest in the brig's earnings—with the salary that the palm-oil people were to pay to me. Indeed, he managed to make me quite discontented with my prospects, although I had thought them very good indeed when I first told him about them; and when he would say jokingly, as he very often did, that I had better drop the palm-oil people and take a berth on the brig instead, I would be half sorry that he was only in fun.

In a serious way, too, he told me that the Coast trade had got very unfairly a bad name that it did not deserve. At one time, he said, a great many hard characters had got into it, and their doings had given it a black reputation that still stuck to it. But in recent years, he explained, it had fallen into the hands of a better class of traders, and its tone had been greatly improved. As a rule, he declared, the West Coast traders were as decent men as would be found anywhere—not saints, perhaps, he said smilingly, but men who played a reasonably square game and who got big money mainly because they took big risks. When I asked him what sort of risks, he answered: "Oh, pretty much all sorts—sometimes your pocket and sometimes your neck," and added that to a man of spirit these risks made half the fun. And then he said that for a man who did not care for that sort of thing it was better to be contented with a safe place and low wages—and asked me how long I expected to stay at Loango, and if I had a better job ahead when my work there was done.

At first he would shift the subject when I tried to make him talk about the slave traffic. But one day—it was toward the end of our second week out, and I was beginning to think from his constant turning to it that perhaps he really might mean to offer me a berth on the brig, and that his offer might be pretty well worth accepting—he all of a sudden spoke out freely and of his own accord. It was true, he said, that sometimes a few blacks were taken aboard by traders, when no other stuff offered for barter, and were carried up to Mogador and there sold for very high prices indeed—for there was a prejudice against the business, and the naval vessels on the Coast tried so persistently to stop it that the risk of capture was great and the profit from a successful venture correspondingly large. But the prejudice, he continued, was really not well-founded. Slavery, of course, was a very bad thing; but there were degrees of badness in it, and since it could not be broken up there was much to be said in favor of any course that would make it less cruel. The blacks who were the slaves of other blacks, or of Portuguese,—and it was only these that the traders bought—were exposed to such barbarous treatment that it was a charity to rescue them from it on almost any terms. Certainly it was for their good, as they had to be in bondage somewhere, to deliver them from such masters by carrying them away to Northern Africa: where the slavery was of so mild and paternal a sort that cruelty almost was unknown. And then he went on to tell me about the kindly relations which he himself had seen existing between slaves and their masters in those parts, both among Arabs and Moors.

This presentment of the case put so new a face on it that at first I could not get my bearings; which I am the less ashamed to own up to because, as I look at the matter now, I perceive how much trouble Captain Luke took to win me for his own purposes—he being a middle-aged man packed full of shrewd worldly wisdom, and I only a fresh young fool.

My hesitation about making up an answer to him—for, while I was sure that in the main point

CAPTAIN LUKE MAKES ME AN OFFER

he was all wrong, I was caught for the moment in his sophisms—made him fancy, I suppose, that he had convinced me; and so was safe to go ahead in the way that he had intended, no doubt, all along. At any rate, without stopping until my slow wits had a chance to get pulled together, he put on a great show of friendly frankness and said that he now knew me well enough to trust me, and so would tell me openly that he himself engaged in the Mogador trade when occasion offered; and that there was more money in it a dozen times over than in all the other trade that he carried on in the *Golden Hind.*

I confess that this avowal completely staggered me, and with a rush brought back all the fears by which I had been so rattled on the first day of our voyage. In a hazy way I perceived that the captain had been playing a part with me, and that the others had been playing parts too—for I could not hope that among men of that stripe such friendliness should be natural—and what with my surprise, and the fresh fright I was thrown into, I was struck fairly dumb.

But Captain Luke—likely enough deceived by his own hopes, as even shrewd men will be sometimes—either did not notice the fluster I was in, or thought to set matters all right with me in his own way; for when he found that I remained silent he took up the talk himself again, and went on to show in detail the profits of a single venture with a live cargo—and his figures were certainly big enough to fire the fancy of any man who was keen for money-getting and who was willing to get his money by rotten ways. And then, when he had finished with this part of the matter, he came out plumply with the offer to give me a mate's rating on board the brig if I would cast in my fortunes with his. Of the theory of seamanship, he said, I already knew more than he did himself; and so much more than either of his mates that he would feel entirely at ease—as he could not with them—in trusting the navigation of the brig in my hands. As to the practical part of the work, that was a matter that with my quickness I would pick up in no time; and my bigness and strength, he added, would come in mighty handily when there was trouble among the crew, as sometimes happened, and in keeping the blacks in order, and in the little fights that now and then were necessary with folks on shore. And then he came to the real kernel of the matter: which was that Bowers did not like his work and was not fit for it, and was threatening to leave the brig at the first port she made, and so a man who could be trusted was badly needed to take his place.

When he had finished with it all I was dumber than ever; for I was in a rage at him for making me such an offer, and at the same time saw pretty

CAPTAIN LUKE MAKES ME AN OFFER

clearly that if I refused it as plumply as he made it we should come to such open enmity that I—being in his power completely—would be in danger of my skin. And so I was glad when he gave me a breathing spell, and the chance to think things over quietly, by telling me that he would not hurry me for answer and that I could take a day or two —or a week or two if I wanted it—in which to make up my mind.

V

I GIVE CAPTAIN LUKE MY ANSWER

For the rest of that day, and for the two days following, Captain Luke did not in any way refer to his offer; and as he showed himself more than ever friendly, and talked away to me in his usual entertaining fashion, my rage and fright began to go off a little—though at bottom, of course, there was no change in my opinions, nor any doubt as to my giving him a point-blank refusal when the issue should be squarely raised.

All this time the brig was bowling along down the trades; and on the third morning after I had the captain's offer—we being then close upon the thirty-fifth parallel of north latitude — Bowers called my attention to the gulf-weed floating about us, and told me that we were fairly on the outer edge of the Sargasso Sea. We should not get into any thicker part of it, he said, as we should bear up to clear it; and so we actually did, hauling away a good deal to the eastward when the brig's course was set that day at noon. But my interest in the matter had been so checked—

I GIVE CAPTAIN LUKE MY ANSWER

all my thought being given to finding some way out of the pickle in which I found myself—that I paid little attention to the patches of yellow weed on the water around us or to the bits of wreckage that we saw now and then; and when Bowers, keeping on with his talk, fell to chaffing me about my desire to make a voyage of discovery into the thick part of this floating mystery I did not rise to his joking, nor did I make him much of a reply.

Indeed, I was in rather a low way that day: which was due in part to my not being able, for all my thinking, to see any sort of a clear course before me; and in part to the fact that the weather was thickening and that my spirits were dulled a good deal by what we call the heaviness of the air. All around the horizon steel-gray clouds were rising, and a soft sort of a haze hung about us and took the life out of the sunshine, and the wind fell away until there was almost nothing of it, and that little fitful—while with the dying out of it the sea began to stir slowly with a long oily swell. Far down to the southeast a line of smoke hung along the horizon, coming from the funnel of some steamer out of sight over the ocean's curve, and the heaviness of the atmosphere was shown by the way that this smoke held close to the surface of the sea.

That Captain Luke did not like the look of things was plain enough from his sharp glances about him and from his frequent examinations of the glass; and he seemed to be all the more bothered—his seaman's instinct that a storm was brewing being at odds with the barometer's prophecy—by the fact that the mercury showed a marked tendency to rise. Had he known as much of the scientific side of navigation as he knew of the practical side he could have reconciled the conduct of the barometer with his own convictions, and so would have been easier in his mind; for it is a fact that the mercury often rises suddenly on the front edge of a storm—that is to say, a little in advance of it—by reason of the air banking up there. But having only his rule-of-thumb knowledge to apply in the premises, the apparent scientific contradiction of his own practical notions as to what was going to happen confused him and made him irritable—the nerve-stirring state of the atmosphere no doubt having also a share in the matter—as was made plain by his sharp quick motions, and by the way in which on the smallest provocation he fell to swearing at the men. And so the day wore itself out to nightfall: with the steel-gray clouds lifting steadily from the horizon toward the zenith, and with the swell of the weed-spattered sea slowly rising, and with a doubting uneasiness among all of us that found its most marked expression in Captain Luke's increasingly savage mood.

Our supper was a glowering one. The captain

I GIVE CAPTAIN LUKE MY ANSWER

had little to say, and that little of a sharp sort, while the mate only rumbled out a curse now and then at the boy who served us; and I myself was in a bitter bad humor as I thought how hard it was on me to be shut up at sea in such vile company, and how I had only myself to blame for getting into it—and found my case all the harder because of my nervous uneasiness due to the coming storm. As to the storm, there no longer could be doubt about it, for the barometer had got into line with Captain Luke's convictions and was falling fast.

When the supper was over the captain brought out his arrack-bottle and took off a full tumbler, which was more than double his usual allowance, and then pushed the liquor across to the mate and me. The mate also took a good pull at it, and I took a fair drink myself in the hope that it would quiet my nerves—but it had exactly the opposite effect and made me both excited and cross. And then we all came on deck together, and all in a rough humor, and Bowers went down into the cabin to have his supper by himself.

What happened in the next half-hour happened so quickly that I cannot give a very clear account of it. A part of it, no doubt, was due to mere chance and angry impulse; but not the whole of it, and I think not the worst of it—for the first thing that the captain did was to order the man who was steering to go forward and to tell the mate to take the wheel. That left just the three of us together at the stern of the brig—with Bowers below and so out of sight and hearing, and with all the crew completely cut off from us and put out of sight and hearing by the rise of the cabin above the deck.

Night had settled down on the ocean, but not darkness. Far off to the eastward the full moon was standing well above the horizon and was fighting her way upward through the clouds—now and then getting enough the better of them to send down a dash of brightness on the water, but for the most part making only a faint twilight through their gloom. The wind still was very light and fitful, but broken by strongish puffs which would heel the brig over a little and send her along sharply for half a mile or so before they died away; and the swell had so risen that we had a long sleepy roll. Up to windward I made out a ship's lights—that seemed to be coming down on us rapidly, from their steady brightening—and I concluded that this must be the steamer from which the smoke had come that I had seen trailing along the horizon through the afternoon; and I even fancied, the night being intensely still, that I could hear across the water the soft purring sound made by the steady churning of her wheel. Somehow it deepened the sullen anger that had hold of me to see so close by a ship having honest

I GIVE CAPTAIN LUKE MY ANSWER

men aboard of her, and to know at the same time how hopelessly fast I was tied to the brig and her dirty crew. I don't mind saying that the tears came to my eyes, for I was both hurt by my sorrow and heavy with my dull rage.

We all three were silent for a matter of ten minutes or so, or it might even have been longer, and then Captain Luke faced around on me suddenly and asked: "Well, have you made up your mind?"

Had I been cooler I should have tried to fence a little, since my only resource—I being caught like a rat in a trap that way—was to try to gain time; but I was all in a quiver, just as I suppose he was, with the excitement of the situation and with the excitement of the thunderous night, and his short sharp question jostled out of my head what few wits I had there and made me throw away my only chance. And so I answered him, just as shortly and as sharply: "Yes, I have."

"Do you mean to join the brig?" he demanded.

"No, I don't," I answered, and stepped a little closer to him and looked him squarely in the eyes.

"I told you so," the mate broke in with his rumble; and I saw that he was whipping a light lashing on the wheel in a way that would hold it steady in case he wanted to let go.

"Better think a minute," said Captain Luke, speaking coolly enough, but still with an angry undertone in his voice. "I've made you a good offer, and I'm ready to stand by it. But if you won't take what I've offered you you'll take something else that you won't like, my fresh young man. In a friendly way, and for your information, I've told you a lot of things that I can't trust to the keeping of any living man who won't chip in with us and take our chances—the bad ones with the good ones—just as they happen to come along. You know too much, now, for me to part company from you while you have a wagging tongue in your head—and so my offer's still open to you. Only there's this about it: if you won't take it, overboard you go."

I had a little gleam of sense at that; for I knew that he spoke in dead earnest, and that the mate stood ready to back him, and that against the two of them I had not much show. And so I tried to play for time, saying: "Well, let me think it over a bit longer. You said there was no hurry and that I might have a week to consider in. I've had only three days, so far. Do you call that square?"

"Squareness be damned," rumbled the mate, and he gave a look aloft and another to windward—the breeze just then had fallen to a mere whisper—and took his hands off the wheel and stepped away from it so that he and the captain were close in front of me, side by side. I stood off from them a little, and got my back against the cabin—that I might be safe against an attack from behind—

I GIVE CAPTAIN LUKE MY ANSWER

and I was so furiously angry that I forgot to be scared.

"Three days is as good as three years," Captain Luke jerked out. "What I want is an answer right now. Will you join the brig—yes or no?"

Somehow I remembered just then seeing our pig killed, when I was a boy—how he ran around the lot with the men after him, and got into a corner and tried to fight them, and was caught in spite of his poor little show of fighting, and was rolled over on his back and had his throat stuck. He was a nice pig, and I had felt sorry for him: thinking that he didn't deserve such treatment, his life having been a respectable one, and he never having done anybody any harm. It all came back to me in a flash, as I settled myself well against the cabin and answered: "No, I won't join you—and you and your brig may go to hell!"

All I remember after that was their rush together upon me, and my hitting out two or three times—getting in one smasher on the mate's jaw that was a comfort to me—and then something hard cracking me on the head, and so stunning me that I knew nothing at all of what happened until I found myself coming up to the surface of the sea, sputtering salt-water and partly tangled in a bunch of gulf-weed, and saw the brig heeling over and sliding fast away from me before a sudden strong draught of wind.

VI

I TIE UP MY BROKEN HEAD, AND TRY TO ATTRACT ATTENTION

My head was tingling with pain, and so buzzy that I had no sense worth speaking of, but just kept myself afloat in an instinctive sort of way by paddling a little with my hands. And I could not see well for what I thought was water in my eyes—until I found that it was blood running down over my forehead from a gash in my scalp that went from the top of my right ear pretty nearly to my crown. Had the blow that made it struck fair it certainly would have finished me; but from the way that the scalp was cut loose the blow must have glanced.

The chill of the water freshened me and brought my senses back a little: for which I was not especially thankful at first, being in such pain and misery that to drown without knowing much about it seemed quite the best thing that I could hope for just then. Indeed, when I began to think again, though not very clearly, I had half a mind to drop my arms to my sides and so go under and have done with it—so despairing was I as I bobbed about

I TIE UP MY BROKEN HEAD

on the swell among the patches of gulf-weed which littered the dark ocean, with the brig drawing away from me rapidly, and no chance of a rescue from her even had she been near at hand.

Whether I had or had not hurried the matter, under I certainly should have gone shortly—for the crack on my head and the loss of blood from it had taken most of my strength out of me, and even with my full strength I could not have kept afloat long—had not a break in the clouds let through a dash of moonlight that gave me another chance. It was only for a moment or two that the moonlight lasted, yet long enough for me to make out within a hundred feet of me a biggish piece of wreckage—which but for that flash I should not have noticed, or in the dimness would have taken only for a bunch of weed.

Near though it was, getting to it was almost more than I could manage; and when at last I did reach it I was so nearly used up that I barely had strength to throw my arms about it and one leg over it, and so hang fast for a good many minutes in a half-swoon of weakness and pain.

But the feel of something solid under me, and the certainty that for a little while at least I was safe from drowning, helped me to pull myself together; and before long some of my strength came back, and a little of my spirit with it, and I went about settling myself more securely on my poor sort of a raft. What I had hit upon, I found, was a good part of a ship's mast; with the yards still holding fast by it and steadying it, and all so clean-looking that it evidently had not been in the water long. The main-top, I saw, would give me a back to lean against and also a little shelter; and in that nook I would be still more secure because the futtock-shrouds made a sort of cage about it and gave me something to catch fast to should the swell of the sea roll me off. So I worked along the mast from where I first had caught hold of it until I got myself stowed away under the main-top: where I had my body fairly out of water, and a chance to rest easily by leaning against the up-standing woodwork, and a good grip with my legs to keep me firm. And it is true, though it don't sound so, that I was almost happy at finding myself so snug and safe there—as it seemed after having nothing under me but the sea.

And then I set myself—my head hurting me cruelly, and the flow of blood still bothering me—to see what I could do in the way of binding up my wound; and made a pretty good job of it, having a big silk handkerchief in my pocket that I folded into a smooth bandage and passed over my crown and under my chin—after first dowsing my head in the cold sea-water, which set the cut to smarting like fury but helped to keep the blood from flowing after the bandage was made fast.

I TIE UP MY BROKEN HEAD

At first, while I was paddling in the water and splashing my way along the mast and while the bandage was flapping about my ears, I had no chance to hear any noises save those little ones close to me which I was making myself. But when I had finished my rough surgery, and leaned back against the top to rest after it—and my heart was beginning to sink with the thought of how utterly desperate my case was, afloat there on the open ocean with a gale coming on—I heard in the deep silence a faint rythmic sound that I recognized instantly as the pulsing of a steamer's engine and the steady churning of her screw. This mere whisper in the darkness was a very little thing to hang a hope upon; but hope did return to me with the conviction that the sound came from the steamer of which I had seen the lights just before I was pitched overboard, and that I had a chance of her passing near enough to me to hear my hail.

I peered eagerly over the waters, trying to make out her lights again and so settle how she was heading; but I could see no lights, though with each passing minute the beating of the screw sounded louder to my straining ears. From that I concluded that she must be coming up behind me and was hid by the top from me; and so, slowly and painfully, I managed to get on my hands and knees on the mast, and then to raise myself until I stood erect and could see over the edge of the top as it rose like a little wall upright—and gave a weak shout of joy as I saw what I was looking for, the three bright points against the blackness, not more than a mile away. And I was all the more hopeful because her red and green lights showed full on each side of the white light on her foremast, and by that I knew that she was heading for me as straight as she could steer.

I gave another little shout—but fainter than the first, for my struggle to get to my feet, and then to hold myself erect as the swell rolled the mast about, made me weak and a little giddy; and I wanted to keep on shouting—but had the sense not to, that I might save my strength for the yells that I should have to give when the steamer got near enough to me for her people to hear my cries. So I stood silent—swaying with the roll of the mast, and with my head throbbing horribly because of my excitement and the strain of holding on there—while I watched her bearing down on me; and making her out so plainly as she got closer that it never occurred to me that I and my bit of mast would not be just as plain to her people as her great bulk was to me.

I don't suppose that she was within a quarter of a mile of me when I began my yelling; but I was too much worked up to wait longer, and the result of my hurry was to make my voice very

I TIE UP MY BROKEN HEAD

hoarse and feeble by the time that she really was within hail. She came dashing along so straight for me that I suddenly got into a tremor of fear that she would run me down; and, indeed, she only cleared me by fifty feet or so—her huge black hull, dotted with the bright lights of her cabin ports, sliding past me so close that she seemed to tower right up over me—and I was near to being swamped, so violently was my mast tossed about by the rush and suck of the water from her big screw. And while she hung over me, and until she was gone past me and clear out of all hearing, I yelled and yelled!

At first I could not believe, so sure had I been of my rescue, that she had left me; and it was not until she was a good half mile away from me, with only the sound of her screw ripping the water, and a faint gleam of light from her after ports showing through the darkness, that I realized that she was gone—and then I grew so sick and dizzy that it is a wonder I did not lose my hold altogether and fall off into the sea. Somehow or another I managed to swing myself down and to seat myself upon the mast again, with my head fairly splitting and with my heart altogether gone: and so rested there, shutting my eyes to hide the sight of my hope vanishing, and as desolate as any man ever was.

Presently, in a dull way, I noticed that I no

VII

I ENCOUNTER A GOOD DOCTOR AND A VIOLENT GALE

I WAS roused from my sleep by the sharp motion of the vessel; but did not get very wide awake, for I felt donsie and there was a dull ringing in my head along with a great dull pain. I had sense enough, though, to perceive that the storm had come, about which Captain Luke and the barometer had been at odds; and to shake a little with a creepy terror as I thought of the short work it would have made with me had I waited for it on my mast. But I was too much hurt to feel anything very keenly, and so heavy that even with the quick short roll of the ship to rouse me I kept pretty much in a doze.

After a while the door of my state-room was opened a little and a man peeped in; and when he saw my open eyes looking at him he came in altogether, giving me a nod and a smile. He was a tall fellow in a blue uniform, with a face that I liked the looks of; and when he spoke to me I liked the sound of his voice.

"You must be after being own cousin to all the

I ENCOUNTER A DOCTOR AND A GALE

Seven Sleepers of Ephesus and the dog too, my big young man," he said, holding fast to the upper berth to steady himself. "You've put in ten solid hours, so far, and you don't seem to be over wide awake yet. Faith, I'd be after backing you to sleep standing, like Father O'Rafferty's old dun cow!"

I did not feel up to answering him, but I managed to grin a little, and he went on: "I'm for thinking that I'd better let that broken head of yours alone till this fool of a ship is sitting still again—instead of trying to teach the porpoises such tricks of rolling and pitching as never entered into their poor brute minds. But you'll do without doctoring for the present, myself having last night sewed up all right and tight for you the bit of your scalp that had fetched away. How does it feel?"

"It hurts," was all that I could answer.

"And small blame to it," said the doctor, and went on: "It's a well-made thick head you have, and its tough you are, my son, not to be killed entirely by such a whack as you got on your brain-box—to say nothing of your fancy for trying to cure it hydropathically by taking it into the sea with you when you were for crossing the Atlantic Ocean on the fag-end of a mast. It's much indeed that you have to learn, I am thinking, both about surgery and about taking care of yourself. But in the former you'll now do well, being in the com-

VII

I ENCOUNTER A GOOD DOCTOR AND A VIOLENT GALE

I was roused from my sleep by the sharp motion of the vessel; but did not get very wide awake, for I felt donsie and there was a dull ringing in my head along with a great dull pain. I had sense enough, though, to perceive that the storm had come, about which Captain Luke and the barometer had been at odds; and to shake a little with a creepy terror as I thought of the short work it would have made with me had I waited for it on my mast. But I was too much hurt to feel anything very keenly, and so heavy that even with the quick short roll of the ship to rouse me I kept pretty much in a doze.

After a while the door of my state-room was opened a little and a man peeped in; and when he saw my open eyes looking at him he came in altogether, giving me a nod and a smile. He was a tall fellow in a blue uniform, with a face that I liked the looks of; and when he spoke to me I liked the sound of his voice.

"You must be after being own cousin to all the

I ENCOUNTER A DOCTOR AND A GALE

Seven Sleepers of Ephesus and the dog too, my big young man," he said, holding fast to the upper berth to steady himself. "You've put in ten solid hours, so far, and you don't seem to be over wide awake yet. Faith, I'd be after backing you to sleep standing, like Father O'Rafferty's old dun cow!"

I did not feel up to answering him, but I managed to grin a little, and he went on: "I'm for thinking that I'd better let that broken head of yours alone till this fool of a ship is sitting still again—instead of trying to teach the porpoises such tricks of rolling and pitching as never entered into their poor brute minds. But you'll do without doctoring for the present, myself having last night sewed up all right and tight for you the bit of your scalp that had fetched away. How does it feel?"

"It hurts," was all that I could answer.

"And small blame to it," said the doctor, and went on: "It's a well-made thick head you have, and its tough you are, my son, not to be killed entirely by such a whack as you got on your brainbox—to say nothing of your fancy for trying to cure it hydropathically by taking it into the sea with you when you were for crossing the Atlantic Ocean on the fag-end of a mast. It's much indeed that you have to learn, I am thinking, both about surgery and about taking care of yourself. But in the former you'll now do well, being in the com-

IN THE SARGASSO SEA

petent hands of a graduate of Dublin University; and in regard to your incompetence in the latter good reason have you for being thankful that the *Hurst Castle* happened to be travelling in these parts last night, and that her third officer is blessed with a pair of extra big ears and so happened to hear you talking to him from out of the depths of the sea.

"But talking isn't now the best thing for you, and some more of the sleep that you're so fond of is—if only the tumbling of the ship will let you have it; so take this powder into that mouth of yours which you opened so wide when you were conversing with us as we went sailing past you, and then stop your present chattering and take all the sleep that you can hold."

With that he put a bitter powder into my mouth, and gave me a drink of water after it—raising me up with a wonderful deftness and gentleness that I might take it, and settling me back again on the pillow in just the way that I wanted to lie. "And now be off again to your friends the Ephesians," he said; "only remember that if you or they—or their dog either, poor beasty—wants anything, it's only needed to touch this electric bell. As to the doggy," he added, with his hand on the door-knob, "tell him to poke at the button with the tip of his foolish nose." And with that he opened the door and went away.

I ENCOUNTER A DOCTOR AND A GALE

All this light friendly talk was such a comfort to me—showing, as it did, along with the good care that I was getting, what kindly people I had fallen among—that in my weak state I cried a little because of my happy thankfulness; and then, my weakness and the powder acting together to lull me, in spite of the ship's sharp motion I went off again to sleep.

But that time my sleep did not last long. In less than an hour, I suppose, the motion became so violent as to shake me awake again—and to give me all that I could do to keep myself from being shot out of my berth upon the floor. Presently the doctor came again, fetching with him one of the cabin stewards to rig the storm-board at the side of my berth and some extra pillows with which to wedge me fast. But though he gave me a lot more of his pleasant chaff to cheer me I could see that his look was anxious, and it seemed to me that the steward was badly scared. Between them they managed to stow me pretty tight in my berth and to make me as comfortable as was possible while everything was in such commotion—with the ship bouncing about like a pea on a hot shovel and all the wood-work grinding and creaking with the sudden lifts and strains.

"It's a baddish gale that's got hold of the old *Hurst Castle*, and that's a fact," the doctor said, when they had finished with me, in answer to the questioning look that he saw in my eyes. "But it's nothing to worry about," he went on; "except that it's hard on you, with that badly broken head of yours, to be tumbled about worse than Mother O'Donohue's pig when they took it to Limerick fair in a cart. So just lie easy there among your pillows, my son; and pretend that it's exercise that you are taking for the good of your liver—which is a torpid and a sluggish organ in the best of us, and always the better for such a shaking as the sea is giving us now. And be remembering that the *Hurst Castle* is a Clyde-built boat, with every plate and rivet in her as good as a Scotsman knows how to make it—and in such matters it's the Sandies who know more than any other men alive. In my own ken she's pulled through storms fit to founder the Giant's Causeway and been none the worse for 'em, and so it's herself that's certain to weather this bit of a gale—which has been at its worst no less than two times this same morning, and therefore by all rule and reason must be for breaking soon.

"And be thinking, too," he added as he was leaving me, "that I'll be coming in to look after you now and then when I have a spare minute—for there are some others, I'm sorry to say, who are after needing me; and as soon as the gale goes down a bit I'll overhaul again that cracked head of yours, and likely be singing you at the same time for your amusement a real Irish song."

I ENCOUNTER A DOCTOR AND A GALE

But not much was there of singing, nor of any other show of lightheartedness, aboard the *Hurst Castle* during the next twelve hours. So far from breaking, the gale—as the doctor had called it, although in reality it was a hurricane—got worse steadily; with only a lull now and then, as though for breath-taking, and then a fiercer rush of wind —before which the ship would reel and shiver, while the grinding of her iron frame and the crunching of her wood-work made a sort of wild chorus of groans and growls. For all my wedging of pillows I was near to flying over the stormboard out of my berth with some of the plunges that she took; and very likely I should have had such a tumble had not the doctor returned again in a little while and with the mattress from the upper berth so covered me as to jam me fast—and how he managed to do this, under the circumstances, I am sure I don't know.

When he had finished my packing he bent down over me—or I could not have heard him—and said: "It's sorry I am for you, my poor boy, for you're getting just now more than your full share of troubles. But we're all in a pickle together, and that's a fact, and the choice between us is small. And I'd be for suggesting that if you know such a thing as a prayer or two you'll never have a finer opportunity for saying them than you have now." And by that, and by the friendly sorrowful look that he gave me, I knew that our peril must be extreme.

I don't like to think of the next few hours: while I lay there packed tight as any mummy, and with no better than a mummy's chances, as it seemed to me, of ever seeing the live world again—terrified by the awful war of the storm and by the confusion of wild noises, and every now and then sharply startled by hearing on the deck above me a fierce crash as something fetched away. It was a bad time, Heaven knows, for everybody; but for me I thought that it was worst of all. For there I was lying in utter helplessness, with the certainty that if the ship foundered there was not a chance for me—since I must drown solitary in my state-room, like a rat drowned in a hole.

VIII

THE *HURST CASTLE* IS DONE FOR

At last, having worn itself out, as sailors say, the storm began to lessen: first showing its weakening by losing its little lulls and fiercer gusts after them, and then dropping from a tempest to a mere gale—that in turn fell slowly to a gentle wind. But even after the wind had fallen, and for a good while after, the ship labored in a tremendous sea.

As I grew easier in my mind and body, and so could think a little, I wondered why my friend the doctor did not come to me; and when at last my door was opened I looked eagerly—my eyes being the only free part of me—to see him come in. But it was the steward who entered, and I had a little sharp pang of disappointment because I missed the face that I wanted to see. However, the man stooped over me, kindly enough, and lifted off the mattress and did his best to make me comfortable; only when I asked him where the doctor was he pretty dismally shook his head.

"It's th' doctor himself is needin' doctorin', poor soul," he answered, "he bein' with his right leg broke, and with his blessed head broke a-most as bad as yours!" And then he told me that when the storm was near ended the doctor had gone on deck to have a look at things, and almost the minute he got there had been knocked over by a falling spar. "For th' old ship's shook a-most to pieces," the man went on; "with th' foremast clean overboard, an' th' mizzen so wobbly that it's dancin' a jig every time she pitches, and everything at rags an' tatters an' loose ends."

"But the doctor?" I asked.

"He says himself, sir, that he's not dangerous, and I s'pose he ought to know. Th' captain an' th' purser together, he orderin' 'em, have set his leg for him; and his head, he says, 'll take care of itself, bein' both thick an' hard. But he's worryin' painful because he can't look after you, sir, an' th' four or five others that got hurt in th' storm. And I can tell you, sir," the man went on, "that all th' ship's company, an' th' passengers on top of 'em, are sick with sorrow that this has happened to him; for there's not a soul ever comes near th' doctor but loves him for his goodness, and we'd all be glad to break our own legs this minute if by that we could be mendin' his!"

The steward spoke very feelingly and earnestly, and with what he said I was in thorough sympathy; for the doctor's care of me and his friendliness had won my heart to him, just as it had won

THE *HURST CASTLE* IS DONE FOR

to him the hearts of all on board. But there was comfort in knowing that he had got off with only a broken leg and a broken head from a peril that so easily might have been the death of him, and of that consolation I made the most—while the steward, who was a handy fellow and pretty well trained as a surgeon's assistant, freshly bandaged my head for me as the doctor had ordered him to do, and so set me much more at my ease. After that, for the rest of the day, he came every hour or so to look after me; giving me some broth to eat and a biscuit, and some medicine that the doctor sent me with the message that it would put strength enough into a dead pig to set him to dancing—by which I knew that even if his head and leg were broken there was no break in his whimsical fun.

The steward was the only man who came near me; but this did not surprise me when he told me more about the condition that the ship was in, and how all hands—excepting himself, who had been detailed because of his knowledge that way to look after the hurt people under the doctor's direction—were hard at work making repairs, with what men there were among the passengers helping too. The ship was not leaking, he said, and this was the luckier because her frame was so strained that it was doubtful if her water-tight compartments would hold; but the foremast had been carried away, and all the weather-boats had been mashed out of all shape or swept overboard, and the mizzen was so shaky that it seemed likely at any moment to fall. Indeed, the mast was in such a bad way, he said, that the first and second officers were for getting rid of it—and of the danger that there was of its coming down all in a heap anyway—by sending it overboard; but that the captain thought it safe to stand now that the sea was getting smooth again, and was setting up jury-stays to hold it until we made the Azores—for which islands our course was laid.

By the time that night came again the sea had pretty well gone down, and beyond the easy roll that was on her the ship had no motion save the steady vibration of her screw. With this comforting change the pain in my head became only a dull heavy aching, and I had a chance to feel how utterly weary I was after the strain of mind and body that had been put on me by the gale. A little after eight o'clock, as I knew by hearing the ship's bell striking—and mighty pleasant it was to hear regularly that orderly sound again—the steward brought me a bowl of broth and propped me up in my berth while I drank it; and cheered me by telling me that the doctor was swearing at his broken leg like a good fellow, and was getting on very well indeed. And then my weariness had its way with me, and I fell off into that deep sleep which comes to a man only when all his energy has slipped away from him on a dead low tide.

THE *HURST CASTLE* IS DONE FOR

How long I slept I do not know. But I do know that I was routed suddenly into wakefulness by a jar that almost pitched me out of my berth, and that an instant later there was a tremendous crash as though the whole deck above me was smashing to pieces, and with this a rattle of light woodwork splintering and the sharp tinkling of breaking glass. For a moment there was silence; and then I heard shouts and screams close by me in the cabin, and a little later a great trampling on deck, and then the screw stopped turning and there was a roar of escaping steam.

I was so heavy with sleep that at first I thought we still were in the storm and that this commotion was a part of it; but as I shook off my drowsiness I got a clearer notion of the situation—remembering what the steward had told me of the condition of the mizzen-mast, and so arriving at the conclusion that it had fetched away bodily and had come crashing through the cabin skylight in its fall. But what the shock was that had sent it flying—unless we had been in collision—I could not understand. And all this while the trampling on deck continued, and out in the cabin the shouts and cries went on.

I thought that the steward would come to me—forgetting that in times of danger men are apt to think only of saving their own skins—and so laid still; being, indeed, so weak and wretched that it did not seem possible to me to do anything else.

IN THE SARGASSO SEA

But he did not come, and at the end of what seemed to me to be a desperately long time—though I doubt if it were more than five minutes—I realized that I must try to do something to help myself; and was the more nerved to action by the fact that there no longer was the sound of voices in the cabin, while the noises on deck a good deal had increased. Indeed, I began to hear up there the puffing and snorting of the donkey-engine, and so felt certain that they were hoisting out the boats.

Somehow or another I managed to get out of my berth, and on my feet, and so to the door; but when I tried to open the door I could not budge it, and in the darkness I struck my head against what seemed to be a bar of wood that stuck in through one of the upper panels and so held it fast. The blow dizzied me, for it took me close to where my cut was and put me into intense pain.

While I stood there, pulling in a weak way at the door-knob and making nothing of it, I heard voices out in the cabin and through my broken door saw a gleam of light. But in the moment that my hope rose it went down again, for I heard some one say quickly and sharply: "It's no good. The way the spar lies we can't get at him—and to cut it through would take an hour."

And then a voice that I recognized for the steward's answered: "But the doctor ordered it.

THE *HURST CASTLE* IS DONE FOR

Where's an axe for a try?" To which the other man answered back again: "If it was the doctor himself we couldn't do it, and we'll tell him so. The ship 'll be down in five minutes. We've got to run for it or the boats 'll be off." And then away they ran together, giving no heed in their fright to my yells after them to come back and not leave me there to drown.

For a little while I was as nearly wild crazy as a man can be and yet have a purpose in his mind. The keen sense of my peril made me strong again. I kicked with my bare feet and pounded with my hands upon the door to break it, I shouted for help to come to me, and I gave out shrill screams of terror such as brutes give in their agony—for I was down to the hard-pan of human nature, and what I felt most strongly was the purely animal longing to keep alive.

But no one answered me, and I could tell by the sounds on deck getting fainter that some of the boats already had put off; and in a little while longer no sound came from the deck of any sort whatever, and by that I knew that all the boats must have got away. And as I realized that I was forsaken, and felt sure from what I had heard that the ship would float for only a few minutes longer, I gave a cry of downright despair—and then I lost track of the whole bad business by tumbling to the floor in the darkness in a dead swoon.

IX

ON THE EDGE OF THE SARGASSO SEA

When I came to myself again, and found my state-room—although the dead-light was set—bright with the light which entered through the broken door, my first feeling was of wonder that I was not yet drowned; for it was evident that the sun must be well up in the heavens to shine so strongly, and therefore that a good many hours must have passed since the smash had happened that had sent everybody flying to the boats believing that the ship was going right down. And my next wonder was caused by the queer way in which the ship was lying—making me fancy at first that I was dizzy again, and my eyes tricking me—with a pitch forward that gave a slope to the floor of my state-room of not less than twenty degrees.

For a while, in a stupid sort of way, I ruminated over these matters; and at last got hold of the simple explanation of them. Evidently, in spite of the straining of the steamer's frame in the storm, her water-tight compartments—or some of them—had held, leaving her floating with her broken bow well down in the water and her stern canted up into the air. And then the farther comforting thought came to me that if she had kept afloat for so many hours already, and seemed so steady in her new position, there was no reason why she should not keep on floating at least for as long as the fine weather lasted—which gave me a chance of rescue by some passing vessel, and so brought a good deal of hope back into my heart.

I still was very weak and shaky, and how I was to get out of the prison that I was in I did not know. By daylight it was easy to see what held me there: which was the end of a yard, with the reef-block hanging to it, smashed through the upper panel and caught so tight in the splintered wood-work as to anchor the door fast. If the wits of the steward and of the other fellow had not been scared clean out of them they easily might have knocked in the lower part of the door with an axe and so opened a way out for me; but as their only notion had been to cut away the spar—a tough piece of work—I could not in cool blood very greatly blame them for having given up my rescue and run for their own lives.

These thoughts went through my head while I lay there, most uncomfortably, on the sloping floor. Presently I managed to get up, but felt so dizzy that I had to seat myself in a hurry on the edge of the berth until my head got steadier. Fortunately my water-jug was half full, and I had a good drink from it which refreshed me greatly; and then I had the farther good fortune to see some biscuit which the steward had left on a shelf in the corner, and as I caught sight of them I realized that I was very hungry indeed. I ate one, along with some more sups of water, and felt much the better for it; but lay down in my berth that I might save the strength it gave me until I should have thought matters over a little and settled some line of action in my mind.

That I was too weak to break the door down was quite certain, and the only other thing that I could think of was cutting out the lower panels and so making a hole through which I could crawl. As this thought came to me I remembered the big jack-knife that had been in my trousers' pocket when I went overboard from the brig; and in a minute I was on my feet—and without feeling any dizziness, this time—and got to where my clothes were hanging on a hook, and found to my joy that my knife and all the other things which had been in my pockets had been returned to them after the clothes had been dried. The knife was badly rusted and I had a hard time opening it; but the rust did not much dull it, and I seated myself upon the floor and fell to slicing away at the soft pine wood with a will. I had to rest now and then, although I found that my strength held out better than I had hoped for, and that put me back a little; but the wood was so soft that in not much more than half an hour I had the job finished—and then I slipped on my trousers, and out I went through the hole on my hands and knees.

I found the cabin in utter wreck: littered everywhere with broken glass and broken wood from the skylight, and from the smashed hanging-racks and the smashed dining-table, and with splinters from the mast—which had broken in falling, and along the whole length of the place had made a tangle of its own fragments and of the ropes and blocks which had held its sails. Of the sails themselves there were left only some fuzzy traces clinging to the bolt-ropes, all the rest having been blown loose and frayed away by the storm. Oddly enough, some of the drinking-glasses still remained unbroken in one of the racks, and with them a bottle partly filled with wine—to the neck of which a card was fastened bearing the name, José Rubio y Salinas, of the passenger to whom it had belonged. I took the liberty of drinking a glass of Don José's wine—feeling sure that he was not coming back to claim it—and felt so much better after it that I thanked him cordially for leaving it there.

Most of the state-room doors stood open, showing within clothing tossed about and trunks with their lids turned back, and the general confusion in which the passengers had left things when they scrambled together their most precious belongings and rushed for the boats—with death, as they fancied, treading close upon their heels. But with what remained in the state-rooms I did not concern myself, being desirous first of all to get on deck and have a look about me that I might size up my chances of keeping alive. That there was no companion-way up from the cabin puzzled me a little, for I knew nothing of the internal arrangements of steamships; but presently I found a passage leading forward, and by that I came to the stair to the deck of which I was in search.

Up it I went, but when I fairly got outside and saw the desperate state of the craft that I was afloat on my heart sank. Indeed, it seemed a flying in the face of all reason that such an utter wreck should float at all. Of the foremast nothing but the splintered stump remained. The starboard rail, which had been to windward of it, was gashed by chance axe-blows made in cutting away the shrouds; and as to the port rail, twenty feet of it was gone entirely where the mast had come crashing down, while the side-plates below were bulged out with the strain put upon them before the standing-rigging fastened there had fetched away. The mizzen-mast lay aft across the cabin skylight, with its standing and running rigging making a tangle on each side of it. The main-mast still stood, but with its top-mast broken off and dangling nearly to the deck. Two of the weather-boats remained fast to the davits, but so smashed that they looked like battered tin wash-basins, and would have floated just about as well. All the other boats were gone: those on the weather side, as the splintered ways and broken ropes showed, having been washed overboard; and those to leeward having been hoisted out by the tackles, which still hung from the davits and dipped lazily with the ship's easy motion into the sea.

All this was bad enough, but what most took the spirit out of me was the way that the ship was lying—her stern high up in the air, and her bow so deep in the water that the sea came up almost to her main-mast along her sloping deck. It seemed inevitable that in another moment she would follow her nose in the start downward that it had made and go straight to the bottom; and each little wave, as it lapped its way aft softly, made me fancy that the plunge had begun.

As to the outlook around me, the only comfort that I got from it was the fairness of the weather and the smoothness of the sea. For close upon the water a soft haze was hanging that even to the north, out of which blew a gentle wind, brought the horizon within a mile of me; and down to leeward the haze was banked so thick that I could make out nothing beyond half a mile. And so, even though a whole fleet might be passing near me, my chances of rescue were very small. But from the look of the ocean I knew that no fleets were likely to be thereabouts, and that even though the haze lifted I might search long and vainly for sight of so much as a single sail. As far as I could see around me the water was covered thickly with gulf-weed, and with this was all sorts of desolate flotsam—planks, and parts of masts, and fragments of ships' timbers — lolling languidly on the soft swell that was running, yet each scrap having behind it its own personal tragedy of death and storm. And this mess of wreckage was so much thicker than I had seen when the brig was on the coast— as Bowers had called it—of the Sargasso Sea as to convince me that already I must be within the borders of that ocean mystery which a little while before I had been so keen for exploring; and my fate seemed sealed to me as I realized that I therefore was in a region which every living ship steered clear of, and into which never any but dead ships came.

X

I TAKE A CHEERFUL VIEW OF A BAD SITUATION

WHEN I perceived the tight fix that I was in my broken head went to throbbing again, and my legs were so shaky under me that I had to sit down on the deck in a hurry in order to save myself from a fall. Indeed, I was in no condition to face even an ordinary trouble, let alone an overwhelming disaster; for what with my loss of blood from the cut on my head, and the little food I had eaten since I got it, I was as weak as a cat.

Luckily I had the sense to realize that I needed the strength which food would give me in order to save myself from dropping off into sheer despair. And with the thought of eating there suddenly woke up in my inside a hungry feeling that surprised me by its sharpness; and instantly put such vigor into my shaky legs that I was up on them in a moment, and off to the companion-way to begin my explorations below. And when, being come to the cabin again, I had another sup of Don José's wine I got quite ravenous, and felt strong enough to kick a door in — if that should be necessary—in order to satisfy my craving for food.

There was no need for staying in doors, for none of them was fastened; but it was some little time —because of my ignorance of the arrangement of steamships—before I could find one that had things to eat on the other side of it. Around the cabin, and along the passage leading forward, were only state-rooms; but just beyond the companion-way I came at last to the pantry—and beyond this again, as I found later, were the store-rooms and the galley. For the moment, however, the pantry gave me all that I wanted. In a covered box I found some loaves of bread, and in a big refrigerator a lot of cold victuals that set my eyes to dancing—two or three roast fowls, part of a big joint of beef, a boiled tongue, and so on; and, what was almost as welcome, in another division of the refrigerator a dozen or more bottles of beer. On the racks above were dishes and glasses, in a locker were knives and forks, and I even found hanging on a hook a corkscrew—and the quickness with which I brought these various things together and made them serve my purposes was a sight to see!

When I had eaten nearly a whole fowl, and had drunk a bottle of beer with it, I felt like another man; and then, pursuing my investigations more leisurely, I found in one of the lockers—which I took the liberty of prying open with a big carving-knife—four or five boxes of capital cigars. In the same locker was a package of safety-matches, and in a moment I was puffing away with such satisfaction that I fairly grew light-hearted—so great is the comfort that comes to a man with good smoking on top of a hearty meal. All sorts of bright fancies came to me: of making one of the battered boats serviceable again and getting off in it, of a ship blown out of her course coming to my rescue, of a strong southerly wind that would carry the hulk of the poor old *Hurst Castle* back again into the inhabited parts of the sea. And with these thoughts cheering me I set myself to work to find out just what I had in the way of provisions aboard my shattered craft.

I did not have to search far nor long to satisfy myself that I had a bigger stock of food by me than I could eat in a dozen years. Forward of the galley were the store-rooms: a cold-room, with a plenty of ice still in it, in which was hanging a great quantity of fresh meat; a wine-room, very well stocked and containing also some cases of tobacco and cigars; and in the other rooms was stuff enough to fit up a big grocery shop on shore—hams and bacon and potted meats, and a great variety of vegetables in tins, and all sorts of sweets and sauces and table-delicacies in tins and in glass. Indeed, although I was full to the chin with the meal that I had just eaten, my mouth fairly watered at sight of all these good things. In the bakery I found only a loaf or two of bread, and this—as it was lying on the floor—I suppose must have been dropped in the scramble while the boats were being provisioned; but in the baker's store-room were a good many cases of fine biscuit, and more than twenty barrels of flour. In addition to all this, I did not doubt that somewhere on board was an equally large store of provisions for the use of the crew; but with that I did not bother myself, being satisfied to fare as a cabin-passenger on the good things which I had found. Finally, two of the big water-tanks still were full—the others, as I inferred from the cocks being open, having been emptied for the supply of the boats; and as a reserve—leaving rain out of the question—I had the ice to fall back upon, of which there was so great a quantity that it alone would last me for a long while. In a word, so far as eating and drinking were concerned, I was as well off as a man could be anywhere—having by me not only all the necessaries of life but most of its luxuries as well.

Finding all these good things cheered me and put heart in me in much the same way that I was cheered and heartened by finding my floating mast after Captain Luke and the mate chucked me overboard. Again I had the certainty that death for a while could not get a chance at me; and this second reprieve was of a more promising sort than

CHEERFUL VIEW OF A BAD SITUATION

that which my mast had given me in the open sea. On board the steamer, or what was left of her, I was sure of being in positive comfort so long as she floated; and my good spirits made me so sanguine that I was confident she would keep on floating until I struck out some plan by which I could get safe away from her, or until rescue came to me by some lucky turn of chance. And so, having completed my tour of inspection, and my general inventory of the property to which by right of survival I had fallen heir, I went on deck again in a very hopeful mood.

Even the utter wreck and confusion into which the steamer had fallen, when I got to the deck and saw it again, did not crush the hope out of me as it did when I came upon it—being then weak and famished—for the first time. I even found a cause for greater hopefulness in observing that the waterline still stood, as it had stood an hour and more earlier, a little forward of the main-mast; for that showed that the water-tight compartments were holding, and that the hulk was in no immediate danger of going down. It did seem, to be sure, that the haze had grown a little thicker, and that the weed and wreckage around the steamer were thicker too; and I was convinced that my hulk was moving — or that the flotsam about it was moving—by seeing a broken boat floating bottom upward that I was sure was not in sight when I went below. But I argued with myself cheerfully that the thickening of the haze might be due to a wind coming down on me that would blow it clean away; and that a small thing like an empty boat drifting down from windward proved that the *Hurst Castle* herself was moving southward very slowly, or perhaps was not moving at all. And so, still in good spirits, I set myself to looking carefully for something that would float me, in case I decided to abandon the hulk and make a dash for it —on the chance of falling in with a passing vessel —out over the open sea.

But when I had made the round of the deck—at least of the part of it that was out of water—I had to admit that getting away from the steamer was a sheer impossibility, unless I might manage it by cobbling together some sort of a raft. It had been all very well for me to fancy, while I was being cheered with chicken and beer and tobacco down in the pantry, that I could make one of the battered boats sea-worthy; but my round of the deck showed me that with all my training in mechanics I never could make one of them float again—for the sea had wrenched and hammered them until they were no better than so much old iron. The raft, certainly, was a possibility. Spars that would serve for its body were lying around in plenty, and with the doors from the rooms below I could deck it over so as to make it both solid and dry; and

CHEERFUL VIEW OF A BAD SITUATION

somewhere aboard the ship, no doubt, were carpenter's tools — though, most likely, they were down under water forward and could be come at only by diving for them. Still, the raft was a possibility; and so was comforting to think about as giving me another reprieve from drowning in case the water-tight compartments broke down — and as that break might come at any moment, and as the job would take me two days at the shortest, I realized that I could not set about it too soon.

XI

MY GOOD SPIRITS ARE WRUNG OUT OF ME

But the other chance which I had thought of, that my hulk might be blown clear of the Sargasso Sea and back into the track of trade again, still was to be reckoned with; and to know how that chance was working it was necessary that I should find out my exact position on the ocean, and then check off the changes in it by fresh observations taken from day to day. And as I saw that the sun was close upon the meridian, and no time to waste if I wanted to secure my first noon-sight, I put off beginning my carpentering until I should have hunted for the ship's instruments and got the latitude and longitude that would give me my departure on my drifting voyage.

This was so simple a piece of work that I anticipated no difficulty in executing it. While the low-lying haze narrowed my horizon it did not sufficiently obscure the sun to interfere with sight-taking; I could count upon finding the chronometers still going, they being made to run for fifty-six hours and the ship having been abandoned only

MY GOOD SPIRITS ARE WRUNG OUT

the night before; and where I found the chronometers I felt sure that I should find also a sextant and a chart. But when I went at this easy-looking task I was brought up with a round turn: there were no chronometers, there was no sextant, there was no chart of the North Atlantic—there was not even a compass left on board!

It took me some little time to arrive at a certainty in this series of negatives. I fancied—because it had been that way aboard the *Golden Hind*—that the captain's room would be one of those opening off from the cabin, and so began my search for it in that quarter. But when I had made the round of all the state-rooms I was satisfied that they had been occupied only by passengers. The single timepiece that I found—for the clock in the cabin had been smashed when the mizzen-mast came down—was a fine gold watch lying in one of the berths partly under the pillow, where its owner must have left it in his hurry to get to the boats. It still was going, and I slipped it into my pocket—feeling that a thing with even that much of life in it would be a comfort to me; but the hour that it gave was a quarter past eleven (it having been set to the ship's time the day before, I suppose) and therefore was of no use to me as a basis for sight-taking.

Having exhausted the possibilities of the cabin I concluded that the captain's quarters must have been forward, and so shifted my search to the forward deck-house; and as I found a blue uniform coat and a suit of oil-skins in the first room that I entered I was sure that in a general way I was on the right track. But in none of these rooms did I find what I was looking for—though I did find in one of them, and greatly to my satisfaction, a chest of carpenter's tools and a big box of nails. The nails must have been there by pure accident, but the tools probably were the carpenter's private kit; and as in the course of my farther search I did not come across the ship's carpenter-shop—which no doubt was under water forward—I felt that this chance supply of what I needed for my raft-building was a very lucky thing for me indeed.

The upper story of the deck-house still remained to be investigated; and when, by the steps leading to the steamer's bridge, I got up there and entered a little room behind the wheel-house, I was pretty sure that at last I had found the place where what I wanted ought to be. The part forward of the doors on each side of this room—a good third of it—was filled by a chart-locker having a dozen or more wide shallow drawers; and the flat top of the locker showed at its four corners the prickings of thumb-tacks which had held the charts open there, and four tacks still were in place with scraps of thick white paper under them—as though some one

MY GOOD SPIRITS ARE WRUNG OUT

in too great a hurry to loosen it properly had ripped the chart away.

This would be, of course, the chart actually in use when the steamer got into trouble, and therefore the one that I needed. As it was gone, I opened the drawers of the locker and looked through them in search of a duplicate; or of anything—even a wind-chart or a current-chart would have answered—that would serve my turn. But while there were charts in plenty of West Indian and of English waters, and a set covering the German Ocean, not a chart of any sort relating to the North Atlantic did I find. Neither were there chronometers nor any nautical instruments in the room. In one corner was a strongly made closet in which they may have been kept; but of this the door stood open and the shelves were bare. Even a barometer which had hung near the closet had been wrenched away, as I could tell by the broken brass gimbals still fast to the brass supports; but this was a matter of no importance, since I had noticed another in good order in the cabin—to say nothing of the fact that my powerlessness to make any provision against bad weather made me indifferent to warnings of coming storms. And then, when I continued my search in the wheel-house, though not very hopefully, all that I discovered there was that the binnacle was empty and that the compass was gone too. In a word, there was absolutely nothing on board the hulk that would enable me to fix my position on the surface of the ocean, or that would guide me should I try the pretty hopeless experiment of going cruising on a raft.

This fact being settled — and hindsight being clearer than foresight—I had no difficulty in accounting for it. In order to lay a course and to keep it, the people in the boats would need precisely the things which had been carried off; and as each boat no doubt had been furnished so that in case of separation it could make its way alone, a clean sweep had been made of all the North Atlantic charts and of all the nautical instruments that the steamer had on board. It was to the credit of the captain that he had kept his wits so well about him—seeing to it, in the sudden skurry for the boats, that the ultimate as well as the immediate safety of his people was provided for—but when I found out, and fairly realized, what his coolness had cost me I fell off once more from good spirits into gloom.

Being left that way all at loose ends as to my reckoning, with no means of finding out where I was nor whether my position changed for the better from day to day, the hopes that I had been building of drifting northward and so falling in with a passing vessel fell down in a bunch and left me miserable. I see now, though I did not see it then, that they went quite as unreasonably as they came. In that region of calms—for I was fairly within the horse-latitudes—the only bit of wind that I was likely to encounter was an eddy from the northeast trades that would set me still farther to the southward; and the only other moving impulse acting upon my hulk—at least while fair weather lasted—would be the slow eddy setting in from the Gulf Stream and moving me in the same direction. In the case of a storm coming up from the south, and so giving me the push northward that I was so eager for, the chances were a thousand to one that my hulk would go to the bottom long before I could get to a part of the ocean where ships were likely to be. And as to navigating a raft through that tangle of weed, already thick enough around me to check the way of a sharply built boat, the notion was so absurd that only a man in my desperate fix would even have thought about it.

But had there been a Job's comforter at hand to put these black thoughts into my head they would not have helped me nor harmed me much. My whole heart had been set on getting my sights, and filled with the inconsequent hope that in getting them I somehow would be bettering my chances of coming out safe at last; and so it seemed to me when I could not get them—and in this, though the sight-taking had nothing to do with it, there was reason in plenty—that all likelihood of my being rescued had slipped away.

I had come out from the wheel-house and was standing on the steamer's bridge—which rose right out of the water so that I looked down from it directly on the weed-laden sea. As far as my sight would carry through the soft golden haze I saw only weed-covered water, broken here and there by a bit of wreckage or by a little open space on which the pale sunshine gleamed. A very gentle swell was running, giving to the ocean the look of some strange sort of meadow with tall grass swaying evenly in an easy wind. The broken boat had moved a good deal and already was well to the south of me; showing me that there was motion in that apparent stillness, and compelling me to believe that my hulk—though less rapidly than the boat—was moving southward too. And what that meant for me I knew. The fair weather might continue almost indefinitely. Days and weeks, even months, might pass, and I still might live on there in bodily safety; but so far as the world was concerned I was dead already—being fairly caught in the slow eddying current which was carrying my hulk steadily and hopelessly into the dense wreck-filled centre of the Sargasso Sea.

XII

I HAVE A FEVER AND SEE VISIONS

Because I had felt hungry and thirsty, and the cold chicken and beer had tasted good, I had eaten and drunk a great deal more heartily than was wholesome for me—being so weakened by loss of blood, and by the strain put upon me by the danger that I had passed through, and by living only on slops and some scraps of biscuit since my rescue, that my insides were in no condition to deal with such a lot of strong food. And then, within an hour after I so unwisely had stuffed myself, came the blow—in itself hard enough to upset a strong digestion in good working order—of discovering that I could do nothing to save myself, and that my hulk was drifting steadily deeper and deeper into that ocean mystery out of which no man ever yet had come alive.

The first sign that I had that something was going wrong with me was a swimming in my head—so sudden and so violent that I lurched forward and was close to pitching over the rail of the bridge into the sea. For a moment I fancied that the ship had taken a quick plunge; and then a sick feeling in my own stomach, and a blurring of my eyes that made everything seem misty and shadowy, settled for me the fact that it was I who was reeling about and that the ship was still—and I had sense enough to lie down at full length on the bridge, between the wheel-house and the rail, where I was safe against rolling off. And then the shadows about me got deeper and blacker, and a horrible sense of oppression came over me, and I seemed to be falling endlessly while myriads of black specks arranged themselves in curious geometrical figures before my eyes—and then the black specks and everything else vanished suddenly, and my consciousness left me with what seemed to me a great crash and bang.

Had I begun matters by being roundly sick I might have pulled through my attack without being much the worse for it. But as that did not happen—my weakness, I suppose, not giving nature a chance to set things right in her own way—I had a good deal more to suffer before I began to mend. After a while I got enough of my senses back to know that my head was aching as though it would split open, and to realize how utterly miserable I was lying there on the bridge with the hot sunshine simmering down on me through the haze; and then to think how delightful it would be if only I were back in the cabin again—where the

I HAVE A FEVER AND SEE VISIONS

sun could not stew me, and where my berth would be easy and soft.

How I managed to get to the cabin I scarcely know. I faintly remember working my way along the bridge on my hands and knees, and going backward down the steps in the same fashion for fear of falling; and of trying to walk upright when I got to the deck, so that I should not get wet above my knees in the water there, and of falling souse into it and getting soaked all over; and then of crawling aft very slowly—stopping now and then because of my pain and dizziness—and down the companion-way and through the passage, and so into the cabin at last; and then, all in my wet clothes, of tumbling anyhow into my berth—and after that there is only a long dead blank.

When I caught up with myself again, night had come and I was in pitch darkness. My head still ached horridly, and I was burning hot all over, and yet from time to time shivering with creeping chills. What I wanted most in the world was a drink of water; but when I tried to get up, in the hope of finding some in the jug that no doubt was in the state-room, I went so dizzy that I had to plump back into my berth again. As the night went on, and I lay there thinking how deliciously the water would taste going cool and sweet down my throat, I got quite crazy with longing for it; and, in a way, really crazy—for through most of the night I was light-headed and saw visions that sometimes comforted me and sometimes made me afraid. The comforting ones were of fresh green meadows with streams running through them, and of shady glens in the woods where springs welled up into little basins surrounded by ferns—just such as I remembered in the woods which bordered the creek where I used to go swimming when I was a boy. The horrible ones were not clear at all, and for that were the more dreadful—being of a fire that was getting nearer and nearer to me, and of a blazing sun that fairly withered me, and of huge hot globes or ponderously vague masses of I knew not what which were coming straight on to crush me and from which I could not get away.

At last I got so worn out with it all that I fell off into an uneasy sleep, which yet was better than no sleep and a little rested me. When I woke again there was enough light in the room for me to see the water-jug, and that gave me strength to get to it—and most blessedly it was nearly full. And so I had a long drink, that for a time checked the heat of my fever; and then I lay down in my berth again, with the jug on the floor at my side.

For a while I was almost comfortable. Then the fever came back, and the visions with it—but no longer so painful as those which had been begotten of my thirst. I seemed to be in a region

I HAVE A FEVER AND SEE VISIONS

dreamy and unreal. Sometimes I would see far stretches of mountain peaks, and sometimes the crowded streets of cities; but for the most part my visions were of the sea—tall ships sailing, and little boats drifting over calm water in moonlight, and black steamers gliding quickly past me; and still more frequently, but always in a calm sea, the broken hulks of wrecked ships with shattered masts and tangled rigging and with dead men lying about their decks, and sometimes with a dead man hanging across the wheel and moving a little with the hulk's motion so that in a horrible sort of way he seemed to be half alive.

Night came again, bringing me more pain and the burning of a stronger fever; and then another day, in which the fever rose still higher and the visions became almost intolerable—because of their intense reality, and of my conviction all the while that they were unreal and that I must be well on the way toward a raving madness in which I would die.

It was at the end of this day—or it may have been at the end of still another day, for I have no clear reckoning of how the time passed—that my worst vision came to me; hurting me not because it was terrifying in itself, but because it made me feel that even hope had parted company with me at last. And it was more like a dream than a vision, seemingly being brought to my sight by my own bodily movement — not something which floated before my eyes as I lay still.

As the afternoon went on my fever increased a good deal; but in a way that was rather pleasant to me, for the pain in my head lessened and I seemed to be getting back my strength. After a while I began to long to get out of the cabin and up on deck, and so have a look around me over the open sea; and with my longing came the feeling that I was strong enough to realize it.

My getting up seemed entirely real and natural, as did my firm walking—without a touch of dizziness—after I fairly was on my feet; and all the rest of it seemed real too. Even when I came to the companion-way I seemed to go up the stairs easily, and to step out on the deck as steadily as though I had been entirely well.

The sun was near setting, but as I came on the deck my back was toward the sunset and I saw only its red light touching the soft swell of the weed-covered sea extending far before me, and the same red light shimmering in the mist and caught up more strongly on a bank of low-lying clouds. The outlook was much the same as that which I had had from the bridge, only the weed seemed to be packed more closely and there was wreckage about me everywhere. Masts and spars and planks were in sight in all directions, sometimes floating singly and sometimes tangled together in little

I HAVE A FEVER AND SEE VISIONS

heaps; half a mile away was what seemed to be a large ship lying bottom upward; near me was a perfectly sound boat, having in its stern-sheets a bit of sail that fell in such folds as to make me think that a human form lay under it; and off toward the horizon was a large raft, with a sort of mast fitted to it, and at the foot of the mast I fancied that I saw a woman in a white robe of some sort stretched out as though asleep. And it seemed to me, though I could not tell why, that all this flotsam, and my own hulk along with it, slowly was drifting closer and closer together; and was packing tighter and tighter in the soft oozy tangle of the weed, which everywhere was matted so thickly that the water did not show at all.

Then I seemed to walk around to the other side of my hulk and to look down into the west—and to feel all hope dying with the sight that I saw there. Far away, under the red mist, across the red gleaming weed and against a sunset sky bloody red, I seemed to see a vast ruinous congregation of wrecks; so far-extending that it was as though all the wrecked ships in the world were lying huddled together there in a miserably desolate company. And with sight of them the certain conviction was borne in upon me that my own wreck presently would take its station in that shattered fleet for which there was no salvation; and that it would lie among them rotting slowly, as they were rotting, through months or years—until finally, in its turn, it would drop down from amidst those lepers of the ocean, and would sink with all its foulness upon it into the black depths beneath the oozy weed.

And I knew, too, that whether I already were dead and went down with it, or saved my life for a while longer by getting aboard of another hulk which still floated, sooner or later my end must come to me in that same way. On one or another of those rotting dead ships my own dead body surely must sink at last.

XIII

I HEAR A STRANGE CRY IN THE NIGHT

THAT was the end of my visions. Through the night that followed — my fever having run its course, I suppose—I slept easily; and when another day came and I woke again my fever was gone. I was pretty weak and ragged, but the cut in my head was healing and no longer hurt me much, and my mind was clear. There still was water left in the jug, and I drank freely and felt the better for it; and toward afternoon I felt so hungry that I managed to get up and go to the pantry on a foraging expedition for something to eat.

This time I was careful not to stuff myself. I found a box of light biscuit and ate a couple of them; and then I filled my water-jug at the tank and brought it and the biscuit back to my stateroom without going on the deck at all. My light meal greatly refreshed me; and in an hour or two I ate another biscuit — and kept on nibbling at them off and on through the night when I happened to wake up. In between whiles my sleep was of a sort to do me good; not deep, but restful. With the coming of another morning I felt so strong that I went to the pantry again for food of a better sort—venturing to eat a part of a tin of meat with my biscuit and to add to my water a little wine; and when this was down I began to feel quite like myself once more, and to long so strongly for some sunshine and fresh air that I climbed up the companion-way to the deck.

But when I got there I thought at first that my visions were coming back again. Indeed, what I saw was so nearly my last vision over again as to make me half believe, later, that I really did go on deck in my delirium and really did see that blood-red sunset and all the rest that had seemed to me a dream. At any rate, there was no doubting this second time—if it were the second time—the reality of what I beheld; and because I no longer was fever-struck, and so could take in fully the wonder of it, my astonishment kept my spirits from being wholly pulled down.

The haze was so thick as to be almost like a fog hanging about me, but the hot sunshine pouring down into it gave it a golden brightness and I could see through it dimly for a good long way; and there was no need for far-seeing to be sure that I had before me what I think must be the strangest sight that the world has in it for the eyes of man. For what I looked at was the host of wrecked ships, the dross of wave and tempest, which through four centuries—from the time when sailors first pushed out upon the great western ocean—has been gathering slowly, and still more slowly wasting, in the central fastnesses of the Sargasso Sea.

The nearest edge of this mass of wreckage was not a quarter of a mile off from me; but it swept away in a great irregular curve to the right and left and vanished into the golden haze softly—and straight ahead I could see it stretching dimly away from me, getting thicker and closer until it seemed to be almost as solid as a real island would have been. And, indeed, it had a good deal the look of being a real island; the loom through the haze of countless broken masts rising to various heights and having frayed ropes streaming from them having much the effect of trees growing there, while the irregularities of the surface made it seem as though little houses were scattered thickly among the trees. But in spite of the golden light which hung over it, and which ought to have given it a cheerful look, it was the most desolate and sorrowful place I ever saw; for it seemed to belong—and in a way really did belong, since every hulk in all that fleet was the slowly wasting dead body of a ship slain by storm or disaster—to that outcast region of mortality in which death has achieved its ugliness but to which the cleansing of a complete dissolution has not yet been brought by time.

Yet the curious interest that I found in this strange sight kept me from feeling only the horror of it. In my talks with Bowers about the old-time sea-wonders which must be hidden in the Sargasso Sea my imagination had been fired; and when I thus found myself actually in the way to see these wonders I half forgot how useless the sight was to me—being myself about the same as killed in the winning of it—and was so full of eagerness to press forward that I grew almost angry because of the infinite slowness with which my hulk drifted on to its place in the ruined ranks.

There was no hurrying my progress. Around me the weed and wreckage were packed so closely that the wonder was that my hulk moved through it at all. Of wind there was not a particle; indeed, as I found later, under that soft golden haze was a dead calm that very rarely in those still latitudes was ruffled by even the faintest breeze. Only a weak swirl of current from the far-off Gulf Stream pushed my hulk onward; and this, I suppose, was helped a little by that attraction of floating bodies for each other which brings chips and leaves together on the surface of even the stillest pool. But a snail goes faster than I was going; and it was only at the end of a full hour of watching that I could see—yet even then could not be quite certain about it—that my position a very little had changed.

Save that now and then I went below and got some solid food into me—and as I was careful to eat but little at a time I got the good of it—I sat there on the deck all day long gazing; and by nightfall my hulk had gone forward by perhaps as much as a hundred yards. But my motion was a steady and direct one, and I saw that if it continued it would end by laying me aboard of a big steamer—having the look of being a cargo-boat—that stood out a little from the others and evidently herself had not long been a part of that broken company. She was less of a wreck, in one way, than my own hulk; for she floated on an even keel and so high out of the water as to show that she had no leak in her; but her masts had been swept clean away and even her funnel and her bridge were gone—as though a sharp-edged sea had sliced like a razor over her and shaved her decks clean.

Immediately beyond this steamer lay a big wooden ship evidently waterlogged; for she lay so low that the whole of her hull, save a bit of her stern, was hidden from me by the steamer, and the most of her that showed was her broken masts. And beyond her again was a jam of wrecks so confused that I could not make out clearly any one of them from the rest. Taken all together, they made a sort of promontory that jutted out from what I may call the main-land of wreckage; and to the right and left of the promontory there went off in long receding lines the coast of that country of despair.

At last the sun sunk away to the horizon, and as it fell off westward pink tones began to show in the clouds there and then to be reflected in the haze; and these tones grew warmer and deeper until I saw just such another blood-red sunset as I had seen in what I had fancied was my dream. And under the crimson haze lay the dead wrecks, looming large in it, with gleams of crimson light striking here and there on spars and masts and giving them the look of being on fire. And then the light faded slowly, through shades of purple and soft pink and warm gray, until at last the blessed darkness came and shut off everything from my tired eyes.

Indeed, I was glad when the darkness fell; for as I sat there looking and looking and feeling the bitter hopelessness of it all, I was well on my way to going crazy with sorrow. But somehow, not seeing any longer the ruin which was so near to me, and of which I knew myself to be a part, it seemed less real to me—and so less dreadful. And being thus eased a little I realized that I was hungry again, and that commonplace natural feeling did me good too.

I HEAR A CRY IN THE NIGHT

I went below to the pantry, striking a match to see my way by; and when I had lighted the big lamp that was hanging there—the glass chimney of which, in some wonderful way, had pulled through the crash which had sent the mizzen-mast flying—the place seemed so cheerful that my desire for supper increased prodigiously, and tended still farther to down my sorrowful thoughts. I even had a notion of trying to light a fire in the galley and cooking over it some of the beef or mutton that I had found in the cold-room; but I gave that up, just then, because I really was too hungry to wait until I could carry through so large a plan.

But there was a plenty of good food in tins easily to be got at; and what was still better I felt quite strong enough to eat a lot of it without hurting myself. I even went at my meal a little daintily, spreading a napkin—that I got from a locker filled with table linen—on the pantry dresser, and setting out on it a tin of chicken and a hunch of cheese and some bread which was pretty stale and hard and a pot of jam to end off with; and from the wine-room I brought a bottle of good Bordeaux.

As I ate my supper, greatly relishing it, the oddness of what I was doing did not occur to me; but often since I have thought how strange was that meal of mine—in that brightly lighted cosey little room, and myself really cheerful over it — in its contrast with the utterly desperate strait in which I was. And I think that the contrast was still sharper, my supper being ended, when I fetched a steamer-chair that I had noticed lying on the floor of the cabin and settled myself in it easily—facing toward the stern, so that the slope of the deck only made the slope of the chair still easier—and so sat there in the brightness smoking a very good cigar.

And after a while — what with my comfort of body, and the good meal in my stomach, and the good wine there too—a soothing drowsiness stole over me, and I had the feeling that in another moment or two I should fall away into a delicious doze. And then, all of a sudden, I was roused wide awake again by hearing faintly, but quite distinctly, a long and piercingly shrill cry.

I fairly jumped from my chair, so greatly was I startled; and for a good while I stood quite still, drawing my breath softly, in waiting wonder for that strange cry to come again. But it did not come again—and as the silence continued I fell to doubting if I had not been asleep, and that this sound which had seemed so real to me had not been only a part of a dream.

XIV

OF MY MEETING WITH A MURDERED MAN

Robinson Crusoe's footprint in the sand did not startle him more than that strange lonely cry startled me. Indeed, as between the two of us, I had rather the worse of it: for Crusoe, at least, knew that he was dealing with a reality, while I could not be certain that I was not dealing with a bit of a dream in which there was no reality at all.

For a long while I sat there puzzling over it— half hoping that I might hear it again, and so be sure of it; and half hoping that I might not hear it, because of the thrilling tone in it which had filled me with a sharp alarm. I was so shaken that I had not the courage to go off to my berth in the cabin, with only a candle to light me there, but stayed on in the little room that the lamp lighted so brightly that there were no dark corners for my fancy to people with things horrible; and so, at last, still scared and puzzled, I went off to sleep in my chair.

When I woke again the lamp had burned out and had filled the place with a vile smell of lamp-smoke that set me to sneezing. But I did not mind that much; for daylight had come, and my nerves were both quieted by sleep and steadied by that confident courage which most men feel—no matter how tight a fix they may be in—when they have the backing of the sun.

My first thought was to get on deck and have a look about me; the feeling being strong in my mind that on one or another of the near-by wrecks I should find the man who had uttered that thrilling cry, and would find him in some trouble that I might be able to help him out of. But my second thought, and it was the wiser, was to eat first of all a good breakfast and so get strength in me that would make me ready to face whatever might come along—for a vague dread hung by me that I was in the way of danger, and whatever it might be I knew that I could the better stand up against it after a hearty meal. Therefore I got out another tin of meat and ate the whole of it, and a hunk of stale bread along with it, and washed down my breakfast with a bottle of beer—longing greatly for a cup of coffee in place of the beer, but being in too much of a hurry to stop for that while I made a fire.

As the food got inside of me—though in that smoky and smelly place eating it was not much of a pleasure—my thoughts took a more cheerful turn. The hope of meeting a live man to talk to

I MEET WITH A MURDERED MAN

and to help me out of my utter loneliness rose strong in my mind; and I felt that no matter who or what he might be—even a man in desperate sickness and pain, whom I must nurse and care for—finding him in that solitude would make my own case less sad. And so, when I went on deck, my longing hope for companionship was the strongest feeling in my heart.

With my first glance around I saw that during the night my hulk had made more progress than I had counted on; having moved the faster, I suppose, as it felt more strongly the pull of the mass of floatage near by. Be this as it may, I found myself so close alongside the big cargo-boat that a good jump would carry me aboard of her; and I was so eager to begin my investigations that I took the jump without a single moment of delay. And being come to her deck, the first thing that I saw there was a dead man lying in the middle of it with a pool of still fresh blood staining the planks by his side.

I never had seen anything like that, and as I looked at the dead man — he was a big strong coarse fellow, dressed in a pair of dirty sail-cloth trousers and in a dirty checked shirt—I went so queasy and giddy that I had to step back a little and lean for a while against the steamer's rail. It was clear enough that he had died fighting. His face had a bad cut on it and there was another on his neck, and his hands were cut cruelly, as though he had caught again and again at a sharp knife in trying to keep it away from him; but the stab that had finished him was in his breast, showing ghastly as he lay on his back with his shirt open—and no doubt it was as the knife went into him there that he had uttered the cry of mortal agony which had come to me through the darkness, with so thrilling a note in it, while I was sitting in bright comfort drowsily smoking my cigar. And then, as I remembered my drowsiness, for a moment I seemed to get back into it—and I had a half hope that perhaps what I was looking at was only a part of a horrible dream.

Had there been any sign of a living man about, of the murderer as well as the murdered, I should have been less broken by what I saw; for then I should have had something practical to attend to—either in bringing the other man to book on the poor dead fellow's account, or in fighting him on my own. But the nearest thing to life in sight, on that storm-swept hulk under the low-hanging golden haze, was the rough body out of which life had but just gone forever; and the bloody stains everywhere on the deck showing that he and another must have been fighting pretty much all over it before they got to an end. And the horror of it all was the stronger because of the awful and hopeless loneliness: with the dead-still weed-covered

I MEET WITH A MURDERED MAN

ocean stretching away to the horizon on the one hand, and on the other only dead ships tangled and crushed together going off in a desolate wilderness that grew fainter—but for its faintness all the more despairing—until it was lost in the dun-gold murky thickness of the haze.

As I got steadier, in a little while, I realized that I must hunt up the other man, the one who had done the killing, and have things out with him. Pretty certainly, his disposition would be to try to kill me; and if I were to have a fight on hand as soon as I fell in with him it was plain that my chances would be all the better for downing him could I take him by surprise. I would have given a good deal just then for a knife, and a good deal more for a pistol; but the best that I could do to arm myself was to take an iron belaying-pin from the rail, and with this in my hand I walked aft to the companion-way—feeling sure that my best chance of coming upon my man unexpectedly was to find him asleep in the cabin below. And then, suddenly, the very uncomfortable thought came to me that there might be more than one man down there—with the likelihood that if I roused them they all would set upon me together and finish me quickly; and this brought me to a halt just within the companion-way, in the shadowy place at the head of the cabin stair.

I stood there for a minute or two listening close-

IN THE SARGASSO SEA

ly, but I heard no sound whatever from below; and presently the dead silence made me feel rather ashamed of myself for being so easily scared. And then I noticed, my eyes having become accustomed to the shadow, that there was a splash of blood on the top step and more blood on the steps lower down—as though a man badly hurt, and without any one to help him, had gone down the stair slowly and had rested on almost every step and bled for a while before he could go on; and seeing this made it seem likely to me that I would have but a single man to deal with, and he in such a state that I need not fear him much. But for all that I kept a tight grip on my belaying-pin, and held it in such a way that I could use it easily, as I put my foot on the first of the bloody steps and so went on down.

The cabin, when I got to it, was but a small one—the boat not being built to carry passengers—and so dusky that I could not make it out well; for the skylight was covered with a tarpaulin—put there, I suppose, to protect it when the gale came on that the steamer was wrecked in—and all the light there was came in from one corner where the covering had fetched away. It gave me a sort of shivering feeling when I looked into that dusky place, where I saw nothing clearly and where there was at least a chance that in another moment I might be fighting for my life.

I MEET WITH A MURDERED MAN

I stood in the doorway, gripping my belaying-pin, until I began to see more clearly—making out that a small fixed table, with a water-jug and some bottles and glasses on it, filled a half of the cabin, and that three state-room doors—one of which stood open—were ranged on each of its sides. And then, just as I was about to enter, I fairly jumped as there came to me softly through the silence a low sad sound that was between a groan and a sigh. But in an instant my reason told me that this was not the sort of sound to come from a man whom I need be afraid of; and as it came plainly enough from the state-room of which the door stood open I stepped briskly over there and looked inside.

XV

I HAVE SOME TALK WITH A MURDERER

At first—the dead-light being fast over the port, and the state-room in darkness save for the little light which came in from the dusky cabin, and my own person in the doorway making it darker still—I was sure of nothing there. But presently I made out a biggish heap of some sort in the lower berth, and then that the heap was a man lying with his back toward me and his face turned to the ship's side.

The noise of my footsteps must have roused him, either from sleep or from the stupor that his hurts had put him in: for while I stood looking at him his body moved a little, and then his head turned slowly and in the shadows I caught the glint of his open eyes. What little light there was being behind me, all that he could see—and that but in black outline—was the figure of a tall man looming in the doorway; but instantly at sight of me he let off a yell as sharp as though I had run a knife into him, and then he covered his head all up with the bedclothes and lay kicking and shaking as though he were in deadly fear.

I HAVE A TALK WITH A MURDERER

I myself was so upset by his outburst, and by the half-horror that came to me at sight of his spasms of terror, that I stood for a moment or so silent; but in one way satisfied, since it was evident that this poor scared wretch could not possibly do me harm. Just as I was about to speak to him, hoping to soothe him a little, he pushed the bedclothes down from over his eyes and took another look at me—and straightway yelled again, and then cried out at me: "Go away, damn you! Go away, damn you! You're dead! You're dead, I tell you! Do you want me to kill you all over again, when I've done it once as well as I know how?" And with that he fell to kicking again, and to shouting out curses, and to letting off the most dreadful shrieks and cries — until suddenly a gasping choking checked him, and he lay silent and still.

Then the notion came to me that he took me for the dead man up on deck; I being about the dead fellow's size and build, and therefore looking very like him as I stood there with the light behind me and the shadows too deep for him to make out my face. And so, to ease his mind and get him quiet—and this was quite as much for my own sake as for his, for his wild fear was strangely horrible to witness—I spoke to him, asking him if he were badly hurt and if I could help him; and at the sound of my voice he gave a long sigh, as though of great relief, and in a moment said: "Who the devil are you, anyway? I thought you was Jack—come back after my killin' him to have another round with me. Is Jack true dead?"

"If you mean the man on deck," I answered, "he is true dead—as dead as any man can be with a cut straight through his heart."

He gave another sigh of relief, as though what I told him was a real comfort to him; and in a moment he said: "Well, that's a good job, and I'm glad of it. He's killed me, too, I reckon; but I'm glad I got in on him first an' fixed him fur his damn starin' at me. Now he's dead I guess he won't stare at me no more." He was silent for nearly a minute, and then he added: "Jest get me a drink, won't you? I'm all burnin' up inside. There's water in th' jug out there. An' put a good dash of gin in it—there's gin out there, too."

I got him some water from the jug on the cabin table, but when he tasted it and found that it was water only he began to swear at me for leaving out the gin; and when I added the gin—thinking that he probably was so used to strong drink as really to need a little to put some life into him—he took off the whole glassful at a gulp and asked for more.

I told him to wait for another drink until I should have a look at his hurts and see what I could do to better them; for, while hanging seemed to be what he deserved, I had a natural desire to ease

I HAVE A TALK WITH A MURDERER

the pain that was racking him—as I could tell by the gasps and groans which he was giving and by the sharp motions which he made.

"Jest shet your head an' gimme some more drink," he said in a surly way. "Jack's give me a dose that 'll settle me, an' lookin' at me won't do no good—'cause there's nothin' to be done. He's ripped me up, Jack has, an' no man can live long that way. All I can do is to die happy—so it's a good thing there's lots of gin. You'll find a kag of it over there in th' fur corner. Me an' Jack filled it from th' spirit-room yesterday, afore our fuss begun."

But I stuck out that I must have a look at his hurts first, and managed to open the dead-light—which luckily had not been screwed tight—and so had some light in the room; and in the end, finding that I would not give him a drink otherwise, he let me have my way. But I had only to take a glance over him to see that what he said about the other man having settled him was true enough; for he was cut in a dozen places savagely, and had one desperate slash—which had laid him all open about the waist—from which alone he was certain to die in a very little while.

There was nothing for me to do, and I did not know what was best to say to him; and while I was casting about in my mind to comfort him a little, for his horrible hurts could not but stir my

IN THE SARGASSO SEA

pity, he settled the matter for both of us in his own way—grunting out that he guessed I'd found he knew what he was talking about, and then asking for more gin.

This time I gave it to him, and gave it to him strong—being certain that he was past hurting by it, and hoping that it might deaden his pain. And presently, when he asked for another drink, I gave him that too.

The liquor did make him easier, and it raised his spirits so much that he fell to swearing quite cheerfully at the man Jack who had given him his death—and seemed to feel a good deal better for freeing his mind that way. And after a while he began of his own accord to tell me about the wreck that he had passed through, and about what had come after it—only stopping now and then to ask for more gin-and-water, and gulping it down with such satisfaction that I gave him all he cared to have. Indeed, it was the only thing that I could do to ease him, and I knew that no matter how much he drank the end shortly would be the same.

As well as I could make out from his rambling talk, the storm that had wrecked him had happened about three months earlier: a tremendous burst of tempest that had sent everything to smash suddenly, and had washed the captain and first and second officers overboard—they all being on the bridge together—and three or four of the crew as

I HAVE A TALK WITH A MURDERER

well. At the same time the funnel was carried away, and such a deluge of water got down to the engine-room that the fires were drowned. This brought the engineers on deck and the coal-passers with them; and the coal-passers—"a beach-combin' lot," he called them—led in breaking into the spirit-room, and before long pretty much all the men of the crew were as drunk as lords. What happened after that for a while he did not know; but when he got sober enough to stagger up on deck he found the man Jack there—who also had just come up after sleeping off his drunk below somewhere—and they had the ship to themselves. The others might have found a boat that would float and tried their luck that way, or they might have been washed overboard. He didn't know what had become of them, and he didn't care. Then the hulk had taken to drifting slowly, and at the end of a month or so had settled into the berth where I found her; and since then the two of them had known that all chance of their getting back into the world again was gone.

"At first I didn't mind it much," he went on, "there bein' lashins to eat aboard, an' more to drink than me an' Jack ever'd hoped to get a show at in all our lives. But pretty soon Jack he begun to be worryin'. He'd get drunk, an' then he'd set an' stare at me like a damn owl—jest a-blinkin' and a-blinkin' his damn eyes. You hev no idee, ontil it's done to you, how worryin' it is when a drunken man jest sets an' stares at you fur hours together in that fool way. I give Jack fair warnin' time and agen when he was sober that I'd hurt him ef he kep' on starin' at me like that; but then he'd get drunk agen right off, an' at it he'd go. I s'pose I wouldn't 'a' minded it in a ornary way an' ashore, or ef we'd had some other folks around. But here we was jest alone—oh, it was terr'ble how much we was alone!—an' Jack more'n half the time like a damn starin' owl, till he a-most druv me wild.

"An' Jack said as how I was onbearable too. *He* said it was me as stared at him—the damn fool not knowin' that I was only a-tryin' to squench his beastly owlin' by lookin' steady at him; an' he said he'd settle me ef I kep' on. An' so things went like that atween us fur days an' days—and all th' time nothin' near us but dead ships with mos' likely dead men fillin' 'em, an' him an' me knowin' we'd soon got to be dead too. An' the stinks out of th' rotten weed, and out of all th' rotten ships whenever a bit of wind breezed up soft from th' s'uthard over th' hull mess of 'em, was horrider than you hev any idee! Gettin' drunk was all there was lef' fur us; and even in gettin' drunk there wasn't no real Christian comfort, 'cause of Jack's damn owlin' stares.

"I guess ef anybody stared steady at you fur

I HAVE A TALK WITH A MURDERER

better'n three months you'd want to kill him too. Anyway, that's how I felt about it; an' I told Jack yesterday—soon as he waked up in th' mornnin', an' while he was plumb sober—that ef he didn't let up on it I'd go fur him sure. An' that fool up an' says it was me done th' starin', and I'd got to stop it or he'd cut out my damn heart—an' them was his very words. An' by noon yesterday he was drunker'n a Dutchman, an' was starin' harder'n ever. An' he kep' at it all along till sunset, an' when we come down into th' cabin to get supper he still was starin'; and after supper—when we mought 'a' been jest like two brothers a-gettin' drunk together on gin-an'-water—he stared wust of all.

"Nobody could 'a' stood it no longer—and up I gets an' goes fur him, keepin' my promise fair an' square. At fust we jest punched each other sort o' friendly with our fists, but after a while Jack give me a clip that roused my dander and I took my knife to him; an' then he took his knife to me. I don't remember jest all about it, but I know we licked away at each other all over th' cabin, an' then up through th' companion-way, an' then all over th' deck—me a-slicin' into him an' him a-slicin' into me all th' time. And at last he got this rippin' cut into me, an' jest then I give him a jab that made him yell like a stuck pig an' down he fell. I knowed he'd done fur me, but somehow I managed to work my way along th' deck an' to get down here to my bunk, where I knowed I'd die easier; an' then things was all black fur a while—ontil all of a sudden you comes along, and I sees you standin' in the door there, an' takes you fur Jack's ghost, an' gets scared th' wust kind. But he's not doin' no ghost racket, Jack ain't. I've settled him an' his damn owl starin'—and it's a good job I have. Gimme some more gin."

And then, having taken the drink that I gave him, he rolled over a little—so that he lay as I found him, with his face turned away from me—and for a good long while he did not speak a word.

XVI

I RID MYSELF OF TWO DEAD MEN

ONLY an hour before I had been longing for any sort of a live man to talk with and so break my loneliness; but having thus found a live man—who, to be sure, was close to being a dead one—I would have been almost ready to get rid of him by going back to my mast in the open sea. Indeed, as I stood there in the shadows beside that dying brute, and with the other brute lying dead on the deck above me, the feeling of dull horror that filled me is more than I can put into words.

I think that the underlying strong strain of my wretchedness was an intense pity for myself. In what the fellow had told me I saw clearly outlined a good deal of what must be my own fate in that vile solitude: which I perceived suddenly must be strewn everywhere with dead men lying unhidden, corrupting openly; since none there were to hide the dead from sight as we hide them in the living world. And I realized that until I myself should be a part of that indecent exhibition of human carcasses—which might not be for a long while, for

IN THE SARGASSO SEA

I was a strong man and not likely to die soon—I should have to dwell in the midst of all that corruption; and always with the knowledge that sooner or later I must take my place in it, and lie with all those unhidden others wasting away slowly in the open light of day. I got so sick as these horrid thoughts pressed upon me that I turned to the table and poured out for myself a stiff drink of gin-and-water—being careful first to rinse the glass well—and I was glad that I thought of it, for it did me good.

My movement about the cabin roused up the dying fellow and he hailed me to give him some more gin. His voice was so thick that I knew that the drink already had fuddled him; and after he had swiped off what I gave him he began to talk again. But the liquor had taken such hold upon him that he called me "Jack," not recognizing me, and evidently fancying that I was his mate—the man whom he had killed.

At first he rambled on about the storm that had wrecked them; and then about their chance of falling in with a passing vessel; and then about some woman named Hannah who would be worrying about him because he did not come home. As well as I could make out he went over in this fashion most of what had happened—and it was little enough, in one way—from the time that the two found themselves alone upon the hulk until they

I RID MYSELF OF TWO DEAD MEN

began to get among the weed, and realized pretty well what that meant for them.

"It ain't no use now, Jack," he rambled on. "It ain't no use now thinkin' about gettin' home, an' Hannah may as well stop lookin' fur me. This is th' Dead Man's Sea we're gettin' into; an' I knows it well, an' you knows it well, both on us havin' heerd it talked about by sailor-men ever sence we come afloat as boys. Down in th' middle of it is all th' old dead wrecks that ever was sence ships begun sailin'; and all th' old dead sailor-men is there too. It's a orful place, Jack, that me an' you's goin' to—more damn orful, I reckon, than we can hev any idee. Gin's all thet's lef' to us, and it's good luck we hev such swashins of it aboard. Here's at you, Jack—an' gimme some more out o' the kag, you damn starin' owl."

There was an angry tone in his voice as he spoke these last words; and the tone was sharper a moment later when he went on: "Can't you keep your owl eyes shet, you beast? Don't look at me like that, or I'll stick a knife into you. No, I'm *not* starin' at you; it's you who's starin' at me, damn you. Stop it! Stop it, I say, you—" and he broke out with a volley of foul names and curses; and partly raised himself, as though he thought that a fight was coming on. And then the pain which this movement caused him made him fall back again with a groan.

IN THE SARGASSO SEA

Without his asking for it I gave him another drink, which quieted him a little; and then put fresh strength into him, so that he burst out again with his curses and abuse. "Cut the heart out of me, will you—you scum of rottenness? I'd have you to know that cuttin' hearts out is a game two can play at. Take that, damn you! An' that! An' that! Them's fur your starin'—you damn fat-faced blinkin' owl. And I mean now t' keep on till I stop you. No more of your owl-starin' fur me! Take it agen, you stinkin' starin' owl. So! An' so! An' so!"

He fairly raised himself up in the berth as he rushed out his words, and at the same time thrust savagely with his right hand as though he had a knife in it. For a minute or more he kept his position, cursing with a strong voice and thrusting all the time. Suddenly he gave a yell of pain and fell on his back again, crying brokenly: "Hell! It's *you* who've finished me!" And then he gave two or three short sharp gasps, and after that there was a little gurgling in his throat, and then he was still—lying there as dead as any man could be.

This quick ending of him came so suddenly that it staggered me; but I must say that my first feeling, when I fairly realized what had happened, was thankfulness that his life was gone—for I had had enough of him to know that having much more of him would drive me mad.

I RID MYSELF OF TWO DEAD MEN

In the telling of it, of course, most of what made all this horrible slips away from me, and it don't seem much to strain a man, after all. But it really was pretty bad: what with the shadowy light in the state-room, for even with the port uncovered it still was dusky; and the horrid smell there; and the vividness with which the fellow somehow managed to make me feel those days and weeks of his half-crazy half-drunken life, while he and the other man stared at each other until neither of them could bear it any longer—and so took to fighting from sheer heart-breaking horror of loneliness and killed each other out of hand. And back of all that I had the feeling that I was caught in the same fate that had shut in upon them; and was even worse off than they had been, since I had no one to fight my life away with but must take it myself when I found my solitude in that rotten desolation more than I could stand.

Even the gin-and-water, though I took another big drink of it, could not hearten me; but it did give me the courage to rid myself of the two dead brutes by casting them overboard; and, indeed, getting rid of them was a necessity, for their presence seemed to me so befouling that I found it hard to breathe.

With the man on deck — except that touching him was hateful to me—I did not have much trouble. I just made fast to him a couple of heavy iron bars that I found down in the engine-room—pokers, they seemed to be, for serving the boiler fires—and then dragged him along the deck to a place where the bulwarks were gone and there shot him overboard. And luckily the weed was thinnish there, and he went down like a stone into it and through it and so disappeared.

But with the man in the cabin I had a harder job. In his horridly cut condition I could not bring myself to touch him, and the best that I could do was to make a sort of bundle of him and the mattress and the bedclothes all together—with a bit of light line whipped around and around the whole mass until it was snug and firm. When it was finished I worked it out of the state-room, and rolled it fairly easily along the floor of the cabin to the companion-way—and there it stuck fast. Budge it I could not; for it was too long to roll up the stair, and too heavy for me to haul it up after me or to push it up before me, though I tried both ways and tried hard. But in the end I managed to get it up by means of a purchase that I rigged from a ring-bolt in the deck just outside the companion-way door; and once having it on deck I could manage it again easily, for there I could roll it along.

Yet I did not at once cast it overboard; for I had no more iron bars with which to weight it, and I knew that such a bunch of stuff would not

I RID MYSELF OF TWO DEAD MEN

sink through the weed—and that I should have it still loathsomely with me, lying only partly hidden in the weed right alongside. In the end I got up a big iron cinder-bucket that I filled with coal—making sure that the coal would stay in it by lashing a piece of canvas over the top—and this I made fast to the bundle by a rope three or four fathoms long. Then I cast the bucket overboard through the break in the bulwarks, and as it shot downward I rolled the bundle after it—and I had the comfort of seeing the whole go down through the weed and away from my sight forever into the hidden water below.

And then I sat down on the deck and rested; for what little cheering and strength I had got from the gin-and-water had left me and I was utterly miserable and tired as a dog. But I was well quit of both my dead men, and that was a good job well done.

XVII

HOW I WALKED MYSELF INTO A MAZE

Sitting there with the splotches of fresh blood on the deck all around me was more than I could stomach for very long. The sight of them brought back to me with a horrid distinctness everything that I had seen since I came aboard the hulk: the dead man lying on the deck, the other man with his frightful wounds and his wild talk and his death in the midst of his passionate ravings, and the disgusting work that I had been forced to do before I could hide their two bodies from my sight in the sea-depths beneath the tangled weed. And so, presently, I scrambled to my feet, thinking to get back to the *Hurst Castle* again—where there was no taint of blood to bring up haunting visions and where, though it seemed a long while past to me, I had been in the company of honest and kindly men.

But when I turned toward this poor escape from my misery—which at best was but a change from a foul prison to a clean one—I saw that I could not easily compass it; for in the time that had

HOW I WALKED MYSELF INTO A MAZE

passed since I had made my jump in the morning—noon being by then upon me—the *Hurst Castle* had swung around a little, being caught I suppose upon some bit of sunken wreckage, so that where the two ships were nearest to each other there was an open reach of twenty feet or more across the weed.

This was too great a distance for a jump, seeing that it must be made from rail to rail without a run to give me a send-off; and yet it was so short that my not being able to cross it never even entered my mind. Had there been a mast standing on the hulk, with a yard fast to it, I could have rigged a rope from the yard-arm and swung myself across in a moment; but the decks being sea-swept, with nothing left standing on them, that way was not open to me; nor could I find a light spar—even the flag-staff at the stern being snapt away—that I could stretch across from one rail to the other and make a bridge of. The only other thing that occurred to me was to tear off some of the doors in the cabin and to make of them a little raft that I could pass by, though I saw well enough that pushing a raft through so dense a tangle even for that short distance would be a hard job. And then I had the thought that perhaps on the sailing-ship lying beside me I might find a sound boat, which would better answer my purpose since it could be the more easily moved through the weed.

IN THE SARGASSO SEA

In point of fact I could not have moved a boat a single foot through that thicket without cutting a passage for it, and I might have thrown overboard three or four doors and so made a bridge over the weed that would have borne me easily—but I did not know then as much about that strange sea-growth as I came to know later on.

As there was no hurry in one way, the ships being so bedded fast there that they were certain not to move more than a few feet at the utmost, I hunted up some food before setting myself to what I knew would be a heavy task; finding cold victuals of a coarse sort in the galley—left from the last meal that the two men had made there—and fairly fresh water in the tank. It was hard work eating, on board that foul ship and thinking of the foul hands which had made the food ready; but going without eating would have been harder, for I had the healthy appetite of a sound young fellow three-and-twenty years old.

When I had finished my meal, and I got through it quickly, I made fast a line to the steamer's rail and slipped down it to the deck of the sailing-ship—a fine vessel of above a thousand tons, built of wood and on clipper lines. There was an immediate sense of relief in getting aboard of her, and away from the blood-stained steamer where the dead men had been; but I saw at a glance that what I was after was not there. She had carried four boats on her rail, as I could tell by the davits, and likely enough a long-boat on her fore-castle as well. But all of them were gone, and I could only hope—since they were not there for my use—that her crew had got safe away in them: as well enough might have happened when she was floating water-logged after the storm that had wrecked her was past.

Without stopping to explore her—and, indeed, after what I had found on the steamer, I had no fancy for explorations which might end in my stumbling upon still more horrors—I went on to a trig little brig lying on the other side of her; a beautiful little vessel, with all her spars and rigging save her bow-hamper in perfect order for sea-going—but showing by her broken bow-sprit that she had been in collision, and by her depth in the water that after the collision she had filled. Naturally enough, her boats were gone too; and so I left her and went on.

In the course of the next two hours or so I must have traversed more than a hundred wrecks—scrambling up or down from one to another, as they happened to lie low in the water or high out of it—and with all their differences of size and build finding them in one way the same: all of them were dead ships which some sort of a sea-disaster had slain. And not one of them had a sound boat left on board. The same reason that kept me from exploring the first of them kept me from exploring any of them: the dread of finding in their shadowy depths grisly horrors in the way of dead men long lying there; and, indeed, I was distinctly warned to hurry away from some of them by the vile stenches which came to me and made my stomach turn sickish and my blood go cold.

I must have walked for a good mile, I suppose, over the dead bodies of these sea-killed ships—and it was the most dismal walk that ever I had taken—before I realized that even if I found a boat and got it overboard it would be of no use to me, since there was no possibility of my getting back in it to my own hulk through that densely packed mass of wrecks and weed. Indeed, I should have perceived this plain certainty sooner had not the wondering curiosity which this strange walk bred in me lured me on and on. And then, being brought at last to a halt by my rational reflection, there came over me suddenly a queer shiver of doubt as to the direction in which the *Hurst Castle* lay; and then a still more shivering doubt as to whether I should be able to get back to her again by the way that I had come, or by any way at all.

At the beginning of my march in this haze-covered sea-wilderness I had tried to keep upon the outer edge of it; but insensibly—having to pass from ship to ship rather by the way that was open to me than by the way that I wished to go—I had

HOW I WALKED MYSELF INTO A MAZE

wandered into the thick of it more and more. And so, when at last I took thought of my whereabouts, and stopped to look around me that I might shape a course back again, I found that in whatever direction I turned I saw only what I had seen ahead of me when my hulk was drawing in upon its borders: a dense confusion of broken and ruined ships which fell away from me vaguely under the golden haze. It had been a dismal sight then; but what gave a fresh note to it, and a thrilling one, was that it no longer was only in front of me but was all around me—stretching away on every side of the wreck on which I was standing, and growing fainter and fainter as the haze shut down thick upon it until it vanished softly into the golden blur.

Yet even then the full meaning of my outlook did not take hold of me. That I was in something of a coil, out of which I could not find my way easily, was plain enough; but that I really was lost in it did not cross my mind. With all my wanderings, I knew that I could not have traversed any great distance; and the certainty that I had passed always from one ship to the ship next touching it seemed to make finding my way back again entirely open and plain. And so I laughed at myself a little—though that was not much of a place for laughter—because of my touch of panic fright; and then I turned back from the ship on which I was standing to the one next to it, over which I had just come—and so on to the next, and in the same way to three or four more. Yet even in that short distance—though my way was unmistakable, for these ships touched only each other as it happened—I was surprised by finding how differently things looked to me as I took my course backward: all the ups and downs of my scrambling walk being inverted, and the lay of the ships one to another and the look of them being entirely changed.

Presently I got on board of a brig—which I well remembered, because it was one of the vessels having about it a vile stench that had made me cross it quickly—on the farther side of which two ships were lying, both rising a little above it and both jammed close against its side. For a moment I hesitated, in doubt as to which of the two I had come by; and I should have hesitated longer had not a whiff of the horrid smell struck upon me strongly and urged me to go on. And so away I went, taking to the ship that I thought was the right one; and still fancying that it was the right one when I got aboard of it—for both, as I have said, were ships, and the two had been about equally mauled by sea and storm. Indeed, except for the differences in their build and rig, there was a strong family resemblance among these storm-broken vessels; and the way that they were jammed together made their build less noticeable,

HOW I WALKED MYSELF INTO A MAZE

while a good many of them were dismasted and so had no rig at all.

Therefore I went on confidently for a dozen ships or more before I had any misgivings that I had missed my way—which was but a natural reaction against my momentary doubtfulness—and then I found myself suddenly pulled up short. Right above me was the side of a big iron steamer—called the *City of Boston*, as I made out from the weathered name-plate on her bows, and a packet-boat as I judged by her build—rising so high out of the water that getting up to her deck was impossible: as equally impossible was my having forgotten it had I made such a rattling jump down. Yet this big steamer was the only vessel in touch with the barque on which I was standing, save the schooner from which I had just come; and that gave me sharply the choice between two conclusions: either I had made that big jump without noticing it, or else—and I felt a queer lump rising in my throat as I faced this alternative—I had managed to go astray completely and had lost myself in what had the look of being a hopeless maze.

XVIII

I FIND THE KEY TO A SEA MYSTERY

ON shore, in a forest, I would not in the least have minded finding myself in a fix of this sort—though my getting into it would have been unlikely—because getting out of it would have been the easiest thing in the world. I know a good deal of wood-craft, and always can steer a course steadily by having the points of the compass fixed for me by the size and the trend of the branches, and by the bark growing thin or thick or by the moss or the lack of moss on the tree-trunks, and by the other such simple forest signs which are the outcome of the affection that there is on the part of things growing for the sun.

But what made my breath come hard and my heart take to pumping—as I stood looking up the tall side of the *City of Boston*, being certain that I never had come down it and so must be off my course entirely—was my conviction that in this forest of the ocean, if I may call it so, there were no signs which would help me to find my way. All around me was the same wild hopeless confu-

I FIND THE KEY TO A SEA MYSTERY

sion of broken wrecks jammed tight together, or only a little separated by narrow spaces thick-grown with weed; and everywhere overhanging it heavily, growing denser the deeper that I got into the tangle, was the haze that made it more confusing still. And under the haze—and because of it, I suppose—was a soft languorish warmth that seemed to steal my strength away and a good deal of my courage too.

But I knew that to give way to the feeling of dull fright, having somehow a touch of awe in it, that was creeping over me would be to put myself into a panic; and that once my wits fairly were addled my chance of getting back to the *Hurst Castle* again would be pretty much gone. And to get back to her seemed to me the only way of keeping my heart up and of keeping myself alive. She was the one ship, in all that great dismal fleet, aboard of which I could be sure that nothing horrible had happened, and in which I could be certain that no loathsome sights were to be come upon suddenly in shadowy nooks and corners to which dying men had crept in their extremity—trying, since none ever would bury them, to hide away a little their own bodies against the time when death should be upon them and corruption should begin.

And so I pulled myself together as well as I could and tried to do a little quiet thinking; and presently I came to the conclusion that I must find my way back to the brig against which the two ships were lying and start afresh from her; since it was pretty certain that it was there, by boarding the wrong ship, that I had got off my course. But because of my certain knowledge of what horridness the brig sheltered, and of the noisome stench that I must encounter there, it took a good deal of resolution to put this plan into practice; so much, indeed, that for a while I wavered about it, and succeeded at last in starting back again only by setting going the full force of my will.

But I need not have whipped myself on to my work so resolutely, nor have fretted myself in advance with planning the rush that I should make across the brig when I came to her—for I never, so far as I know, laid eyes on her again. For a little while, as in my first turn-about, I found my way backward without much difficulty—though again the different look that the ships had as I returned across them pulled me up from time to time with doubts about them; and then, just as before, I came to a place where more than one line of advance was open to me and there went wrong—as I knew a little later by finding myself aboard a vessel so strange in her appearance that my first glimpse over her deck satisfied me that I saw her then for the first time.

This craft was an old-fashioned sloop-of-war,

I FIND THE KEY TO A SEA MYSTERY

carrying eighteen guns; and that she had perished in action was as evident as that her death-battle had been fought a long while back in the past. The mauling that she had received had made an utter wreck of her—her masts being shot away and hanging by the board, most of her bulwarks being splintered, and her whole stern torn open as though a crashing broad-side had been poured into her at short range. Moreover, nearly all her guns had been dismounted, and two of them had burst in firing—as the shattered gun-carriages showed.

But what most strongly proved the fierceness of her last action, and the length of time that had passed since she fought it, were the scores of skeletons lying about her deck — a few with bits of clothing hanging fast to them, but most of them clean fleshless naked bones. Just as they had fallen, there they lay: with legs or arms or ribs splintered or carried off by the shot which had struck them, or with bullet-holes clean through their skulls. But the sight of them, while it put a sort of awe upon me, did not horrify me; because time had done its cleansing work with them and they were pure.

Indeed, my imagination was taken such fast hold of by coming upon this thrilling wreck of ancient sea-battle, fought out fiercely to a finish generations before ever I was born, that for a little while I forgot my own troubles entirely; and so got over the shock which my first sight of the riddled sloop and her dead crew had given me by proving that again I had lost my way. And my longing to know all that I could find out about it—backed by the certainty that I should not come upon anything below that would revolt me—led me to go searching in the shattered cabin for some clue to the sloop's name and nationality, and to the cause in which her death-fight had been fought.

The question of nationality was decided the moment that I set my foot within the cabin doorway —there being a good deal of light there, coming in through the broken stern—by my seeing stretched over a standing bed-place in a state-room to starboard an American flag; and the flag, taken together with the ancient build of the sloop, also settled the fact pretty clearly that the action which had finished her must have been fought with an English vessel in the War of 1812.

Under the flag I could make out faintly the lines of a human figure, and I knew that one of the sloop's officers—most likely her commander, from the respect shown to him by covering him with the colors—must be lying there, just as his men had placed him to wait for a sea-burial until the fighting should come to an end. And that he had remained there was proof that not a man of the sloop's company but had been killed outright in the fight or had got his death-wound in it; and also

I FIND THE KEY TO A SEA MYSTERY

of the fact that in a way the fight had been a victory—since it was evident that the enemy had not taken possession, and therefore must have been beaten off.

But the whole matter was settled clearly by my finding the sloop's log-book lying open on the cabin table, just as it had lain there, and had entries made in it, while the action was going on. And a very strange thrill ran through me as I read on the mouldy page in brown faint letters the date, "October 5, 1814," and across the page-head, in bigger brown faint letters: "U. S. Sloop-of-war *Wasp*": and so knew that I was aboard of that stinging little war-sloop—whereof the record is a bright legend, and the fate a mystery, of our Navy —which in less than three months' time successively fought and whipped three English war-vessels— the ship *Reindeer* and the brigs *Avon* and *Atalanta*, all of them bigger than herself—and then, being last sighted in September, 1814, not far from the Azores, vanished with all her crew and officers from off the ocean and never was seen nor heard of again.

There before me in the mouldy log-book was the record of her last action—and in gallantry it led the three others which have made her fame.

The entries began at 7.20 A.M. with: "A strange sail in sight on the weather bow;" at 7.45 followed: "The strange brig bearing down on us. Looks

IN THE SARGASSO SEA

English"; and at 8.10: "The strange brig has shown English colors." Then came the manœuvring for position, covering more than an hour, and the beating to general quarters; and after that the short entries ran on quickly—in such rough and ready writing as might be expected of a man dashing in for a moment to make them, and then dashing out again to where the fighting was going on:

"9.20 A.M. Engaged the enemy with our starboard battery, hulling him severely.

"9.24. Our foremast by the board.

"9.28. The enemy's broadside in our stern. Great havoc.

"9.35. The wreck of the foremast cleared, giving us steerage way.

"9.40. Our hulling fire telling. The enemy's battery fire slacking. His musketry fire very hot and galling.

"9.45. The enemy badly hulled. More than half of our crew now killed or disabled.

"9.52. Our main-mast by the board and our mizzen badly wounded. Action again very severe. Few of our men left.

"9.56. Captain Blakeley killed and brought below.

"10.01. Our mizzen down. The enemy's fire slacking again.

"10.10. The enemy sheering off, with the look of being sinking.

"10.15. The enemy sinking. We cannot help him. Most of our men are dead. All of us living are badly hurt."

And there the entries came to an end.

My breath came fast as I read that short record of as brave a fight as ever was fought on salt water;

I FIND THE KEY TO A SEA MYSTERY

and when my reading was finished I gave a great sigh. It was a fit ending for the little *Wasp*, that death triumphant: and it was a fit ending to a fight between American and English sailors that they should hang at each other's throats, neither yielding, until they died that way — they being each of a nation unaccustomed to surrender, and both of the one race which alone in modern times has held the sea.

XIX

OF A GOOD PLAN THAT WENT WRONG WITH ME

For a while I was so stirred by the enthusiasm which my discovery aroused in me that I had no room in my mind for any other thoughts. But at last, as I still stood pondering in the *Wasp's* cabin, I became aware that the daylight was fading into darkness; and as I realized what that meant for me my thoughts came back suddenly to myself, and then all my enthusiasm ebbed away.

I came out upon the deck again, but leaving everything as I had found it—my momentary impulse to lift the flag having vanished as I felt how fit it was that this dead battle-captain should rest on undisturbed where his men had laid him beneath the colors that he had died for; and I was glad to find when I got into the open that a good deal of daylight still remained. But it was so far gone, and was waning so rapidly, that I saw that I had little chance of getting back to the *Hurst Castle* before nightfall; and that the most that I could hope for was to make a start in the right direction —and perhaps to find a wreck to sleep on that had

A GOOD PLAN THAT WENT WRONG

food and water aboard of it, and thence take up my search again the next day.

Yet the dread was strong upon me, as I looked around upon the wrecks among which the *Wasp* was bedded, that I might not only be unable to find the *Hurst Castle* again, but ever to find my way across that tangle to the outer edges of it—where only was it possible that ships on which were provisions fit for eating would be found. The very fact that the *Wasp* had settled into her position more than fourscore years back made it certain that she was deep in the labyrinth; and the strange old-fashioned look of the craft surrounding her showed me that I should have to go far before finding a vessel wrecked in recent times.

But these disheartening thoughts I crushed down as well as I could, yet not making much of it; and as trying to go back by the way that I had come to the *Wasp* would not serve any good purpose—even supposing that I could have managed it, which was not likely—I went on beyond her on a new course: taking a longish jump from her quarter-rail and landing on the deck of a clumsy little ill-shapen brig, with a high-built square stern and a high-built bow that was pretty nearly square too. She was Dutch, I fancy, and a merchant vessel; but she carried a little battery of brass six-pounders, and had also a half dozen pederaros set along her rail. And by her carrying these old-fashioned swivel-guns—which proved that she had got her armament not much later than the middle of the last century — and by the general look of her, I knew that she was an older vessel even than the *Wasp*.

This observation, and the reflection growing out of it that the deeper I went into the Sargasso Sea the older must be the craft bedded in it—since that great dead fleet is recruited constantly by new wrecks drifting in upon its outer edges from all ways seaward—put into my head what seemed to me to be a very reasonable plan for finding my way back to the *Hurst Castle* again; or, at least, to some other newly come in hulk on which there would be fresh water and sound food. And this was to shape my course by considering attentively the look of each wreck that I came aboard of, and the look of those surrounding it, and by then going forward to whichever one of them seemed to be of the most modern build.

As the first step in carrying out my plan—and it seemed to be such a good plan that I felt almost light-hearted over it—I got up on the rail of the old brig and jumped back to the less-old *Wasp* again: landing in her main-channels, and thence easily boarding her by scrambling up what was left of the chains. But in taking my next step I had no choice in the matter, as only one other vessel was in touch with the sloop—a heavily-built little schooner that had the look of being quite as old as the brig which I had just left. And her age was so evident as I came aboard of her—having crossed the deck of the *Wasp* hastily, picking my way among the scattered bones—that of a sudden my faith in my fine plan for getting out of the tangle began to wane.

In a general way, of course, the conclusion which I had arrived at was a sound one. Broadly speaking, it was certain that could I pass in a straight line from the centre to the circumference of that vast assemblage of wrecks I constantly would find vessels of newer build; and so at last, upon the outermost fringe, would come to the wrecks of ships belonging to my own day. But one weak point in my calculations was my inability to hold to a straight line, or to anything like one—because I had to advance from one wreck to another as they happened to touch or to be within jumping distance of each other, and therefore went crookedly upon my course and often fairly had to double on it. And another weak point was that the sea in its tempests recognizes no order of seniority, but destroys in the same breath of storm ships just beginning their lives upon it and ships which have withstood its ragings for a hundred years: so that I very well might find—as I actually did find in the case of the *Wasp*—a comparatively modern-built vessel lying hemmed in by ancient craft, survivals of obsolete types, which had lingered so long upon the ocean that in their lives as in their deaths they merged and blended the present and the past.

Thus a check was put upon my plan at the very outset; yet in a stolid sort of way—knowing that to give it up entirely would be to bring despair upon me, for I could not think of a better one—I tried still to hold by it: going on from the clumsy little old schooner to that one of two vessels lying beyond her which I fancied, though both of them belonged to a long past period, was the more modern-looking in her build. And so I continued to go onward over a dozen craft of one sort or another, holding by my rule—or trying to believe that I was holding by it, for all of the wrecks which I crossed were of an antique type—and now and then being left with no chance for choosing by finding open to me only a single way. And all this while the daylight was leaving me—the sun having gone down a ruddy globe beyond the forest of wrecks westward, and heavy purple shadows having begun to close down upon me through the low-hanging haze.

The imminence of night-fall made clear to me that I had no chance whatever of getting out from among those long-dead ships before the next morning; and this certainty was the harder to bear because I was desperately hungry — more than six hours having passed since I had eaten anything—and thirsty too: though my thirst, because of the dampness of the haze I suppose, was not very severe. But the belief that I really was advancing toward the coast of my strange floating continent and that I should find both food and drink when I got there, made me press forward; comforting myself as well as I could with the reflection that even though I did have to keep a hungry and thirsty vigil among those old withered hulks I yet should be the nearer, by every one of them that I put behind me that night, to the freshly come in wrecks on the coast line—where I made sure of finding a breakfast on the following day. Moreover, I knew how forlornly miserable I should be the moment that I lost the excitement of scrambling and climbing and just sat down there among the ancient dead, with the darkness closing over me, to wait for the slow coming of another day. And my dread of that desolate loneliness urged me to push forward while the least bit of daylight was left by which to see my way.

It was ticklish work, as the dusk deepened, getting from one wreck to another; and at last—after nearly going down into the weed between two of them, because of a rotten belaying-pin that I caught at breaking in my hand—I had to resign myself to giving over until morning any farther attempt to advance. But I was cheered by the thought that I had got on a good way in the hour or more that had gone since I had left the *Wasp* behind me; and so I tried to make the best of things as I cast around me for some sheltered nook on the deck of the vessel I had come aboard of—a little clumsy old brig—where my night might be passed. As to going below, either into the cabin or the forecastle, I could not bring myself to it; for my heart failed me at the thought of what I might touch in the darkness there, and my mind—sore and troubled by all that I had passed through, and by the dim dread filling it—certainly would have crowded those black depths with grisly phantoms until I very well might have gone mad.

And so, as I say, I cast about the deck of the brig for some nook that would shelter me from the dampness while I did my best to sleep away into forgetfulness my hunger and my thirst; but was troubled all the while that I was making my round of investigation by a haunting feeling that I had been on that same deck only a little while before. Growing stronger and stronger, this feeling became so insistent that I could not rest for it; and presently compelled me to try to quiet it by taking a look at the wreck next beyond the brig to see if I recognized that too—as would be likely, since I must have crossed it also, had I really come that way.

I did not try to board this adjoining wreck, but only clambered up on the rail of the brig so that I could look well at it—and when I got my look I came more nearly to breaking down completely than I had done at any time since I had been cast overboard from the *Golden Hind*. For there, showing faintly in the gloom below me, was the gun-set deck of a war-ship, and over the deck dimly-gleaming bones were scattered—and in that moment I knew that the whole of my wandering had been but a circle, and that I was come back again at the weary ending of it to the *Wasp*.

But what crushed the heart of me was not that my afternoon of toil had been wasted, but the strong conviction—from which I no longer saw any way of escaping—that I had strayed too deep into that hideous sea-labyrinth ever to find my way out of it, and that I must die there slowly for lack of water and of food.

XX

HOW I SPENT A NIGHT WEARILY

I got down from the rail and seated myself on the brig's deck, leaning my back against her bulwarks and a little sheltered by their old-fashioned in-board overhang. But I had no very clear notion of what I was doing; and my feeling, so far as I had any feeling, was less that I was moving of my own volition than that I was being moved by some power acting from outside of me—the sensation of irresponsibility that comes to one sometimes in a dream.

Indeed, the whole of that night seemed to me then, and still seems to me, much more a dream than a reality: I being utterly wearied by my long hard day's work in scrambling about among the wrecks, and a little light-headed because of my stomach's emptiness, and feverish because of my growing thirst, and my mind stunned by the dull pain of my despair. And it was lucky for me, I suppose, that my thinking powers were so feeble and so blunted. Had I been fully awake to my own misery I might very well have gone crazy

HOW I SPENT A NIGHT WEARILY

there in the darkness; or have been moved by a sharp horror of my surroundings to try to escape them by going on through the black night from ship to ship—which would have ended quickly by my falling down the side of one or another of them and so drowning beneath the weed.

Yet the sort of stupor that I was in did not hold fast my inner consciousness; being rather a numbing cloud surrounding me and separating me from things external—though not cutting me off from them wholly — while within this wrapping my spirit in a way was awake and free. And the result of my being thus on something less than speaking terms with my own body was to make my attitude toward it that of a sympathizing acquaintance, with merely a lively pity for its ill-being, rather than that of a personal partaker in its pains. And even my mental attitude toward myself was a good deal of the same sort: for my thoughts kept turning sorrowfully to the sorrow of my own spirit solitary there, shrinking within itself because of its chill forsakenness and lonely pain of finding itself so desolate — the one thing living in that great sea-garnering of the dead.

And after a while — either because my light-headedness increased, or because I dozed and took to dreaming — I had the feeling that the dense blackness about me, a gloom that the heavily overhanging mist made almost palpable, was filling with all those dead spirits come to peer curiously into my living spirit; and that they hated it and were envious of it because it was not as they were but still was alive. And from this, presently, I went on to fancying that I could see them about me clad again dimly in the forms which had clothed them when they also in their time had been living men. At first they were uncertain and shadowy, but before long they became so distinct that I plainly saw them: shaggy-bearded resolute fellows, roughly dressed in strange old-fashioned sea-gear, with here and there among them others in finer garb having the still more resolute air of officers; and all with the fierce determined look of those old-time mariners of the period when all the ocean was a battling-place where seamen spent their time—and most of them, in the end, spent their lives also—in fighting with each other and in fighting with the sea.

Gradually this throng of the sea-dead filled the whole deck about me and everywhere hemmed me in; but they gave no heed to me, and were ranged orderly at their stations as though the service of the ship was being carried on. Among themselves they seemed to talk; but I could hear nothing of what they were saying, though I fancied that there was a humming sound filling the air about me like the murmur of a far-away crowd. Now and then an angry bout would spring up suddenly between two or three of them; and in a moment they would be fighting together, and would keep at it until one of their stern officers was upon them with blows right and left with his fists or with the butt of his pistol or with the pommel of his sword—and so would scatter the rough brutes, scowling, and as it seemed uttering growls such as beasts lashed by their keepers would give forth.

And at other times they would seem to be fighting with some enemy — serving at their guns stripped half-naked, with handkerchiefs knotted about their heads, and with the grime of powder-smoke upon their bare flesh and so blackening their faces as to give their gleaming eyes a still more savage look; falling dead or wounded with their blood streaming out upon the deck and making slimy pools in which a man running sometimes would slip and go down headlong—and would get up, with a laugh and a curse, only in another moment to drop for good as a musket-ball struck him or as a round-shot sliced him in two; and all of them with a savage joy in their work, and going at it with a lust for blood that made them delight in it—and take no more thought than any other fighting brutes would take of guarding their own lives.

Or, again, they would seem to be in the midst of a tempest, with the roar of the wind and the rush of the waves upon them, and would be fighting the gale and the ocean's turbulence with the same devil's daring that they had shown in fighting the enemy — and with the same carelessness as to what happened to themselves so long as they stuck to their duty and did the best that was in them to bring their ship safely through the storm. And so they went on ringing the changes on their old-time wild sea-life—their savage fights among themselves, and their battlings with foemen of a like metal, and their warfare with the ocean— while the dark night wore on.

Yet even when these visionary forms were thickest about me—and when it seemed, too, as though from all the dead hulks about me the shadows of the dead were rising in the same fashion in pale fierce throngs—I tried to hold fast, and pretty well succeeded in it, to the steadying conviction that the making of them was in my own imagination and that they were not real. And then, too, I fell off from time to time into a light sleep which still was deep enough to rid me of them wholly; and which also gave me some of the rest that I so much needed after all that I had passed through during that weary day.

What I could not get rid of, either sleeping or waking, was my gnawing hunger and my still worse thirst. For an hour or two after nightfall, the air being fresher and the haze turning to a damp cool mist, my thirst was a good deal les-

HOW I SPENT A NIGHT WEARILY

sened; which was a gain in one way, though not in another—for that same chill of night very searchingly quickened my longing for food. But as the hours wore away my desire for water got the better of every other feeling, even changing my haunting visions of dead crews rising from the dead ships about me into visions of brooks and rivulets —which only made my burning craving the more keen.

Nor did what little reasoning I could bring to bear upon my case, when from time to time I partly came out from the sort of lethargy that had hold of me, do much for my comforting. It was possible, I perceived, that I might find even in a long-wrecked ship some half-rotten scraps of old salted meat, or some remnant of musty flour, that at least would serve to keep life in me. But even food of this wretched sort would do me no good without water—and water was to be found only in one of the wrecks forming the outer fringe of my prison, toward which I had been trying so long vainly to find my way.

Yet in spite of my having already gone astray half a dozen times over in daylight I still did have, deep down in me, a feeling that if only the darkness would pass I could manage to steer a true course. And when at last, as it seemed to me after years of waiting for it, I began to see a little pink tone showing in the mist dimly it almost seemed as though my troubles were coming instantly to an end. And, at least, the horror of deep darkness, which all night long had been crushing me, did leave me from the moment when that first gleam of returning daylight appeared.

XXI

MY THIRST IS QUENCHED, AND I FIND A COMPASS

It was a long while before the pale pink gleam to the eastward spread up into the sky far enough to thin the shadows which hung over my dead fleet heavily, and longer still before I had light enough to venture to begin my scrambling walk from ship to ship again. It seemed to me, indeed, that the mist lay lower and was a good deal thicker than on the preceding evening; and this, with the fiery glow that was in it when the sunrise came, gave me hope that a douse of rain might be coming — which chance of getting the water that I longed for heartened me even more than did the up-coming of the sun.

My throat was hurting me a good deal because of its dryness, and my itching thirst was all the stronger because the last food I had eaten—being the mess left in the pan by the two men who had killed each other—had been a salt-meat stew. Of hunger I did not feel much, save for gripes in my inside now and then; but I was weak because of my emptiness—as I discovered when I got on my legs, and found myself staggering a little and the things around me swimming before my eyes. And what was worse than that was a dull stupidity which so possessed me that I could not think clearly; and so for a while kept me wandering about the deck of the brig aimlessly, while my wits went wool-gathering instead of trying to work out some plan—even a foolish plan—which would cheer me up with hopes of pulling through.

I might have gone on all day that way, very likely, if I had not been aroused suddenly by feeling a big drop of rain on my face; and only a moment later—the thick mist, I suppose, being surcharged with water, and some little waft of wind in its upper region having loosened its vent-peg—I was in the thick of a dashing shower. So violent was the downpour that in less than a minute the deck was streaming, and I had only to plug with my shirt one of the scuppers amidships to have in another minute or two a little lake of fresh sweet water from which—lying on my belly, with the rain pelting down on me—I drank and drank until at last I was full. And the feel of the rain on my body was almost as good as the drinking of it, for it was deliciously cool and yet not chill.

When I got at last to my legs again, with the dryness gone from my throat and only a little pain there because of the swollen glands, I found that I walked steadily and that my head was clear too;

and for the moment I was so entirely filled with water that I was not hungry at all. Presently the rain stopped, and that set me to thinking of finding some better way to keep a store of water by me than leaving it in a pool on the open deck; where, indeed, it would not stay long, but would ooze out through the scupper and be sopped up by the rotten planks.

And so, though I did not at all fancy going below on the old brig, I went down the companion-way into the cabin to search for a vessel of some sort that would be water-tight; and shivered a little as I entered that dusky place, and did not venture to move about there until my eyes got accustomed to the half darkness for fear that I should go stumbling over dead men's bones.

As it turned out, the cabin was bare enough of dead people, and of pretty much everything else; from which I inferred that in the long past time when the brig had been wrecked her crew had got safe away from her, and had been able in part to strip her before they left her alone upon the sea. What I wanted, however, they had not taken away. In a locker I found a case made to hold six big bottles, in which the skipper had carried his private stock of liquors very likely; and two of the bottles, no doubt being empty when the cabin was cleared, had been left behind. They served my turn exactly, and I brought them on deck and filled them from my pool of rain-water—and so was safe against thirst for at least another day.

Being thus freshened by my good drink, and cheered by the certainty of having water by me, I sat down for a while on the cabin-scuttle that I might puzzle out a plan for getting to some ship so recently storm-slain that aboard of her still would be eatable food. As for rummaging in the hold of the brig, I knew that no good could come of it—she having lain there, as I judged, for a good deal more than half a century; and for the same reason I knew that I only would waste time in searching the other old wrecks about me for stores. All that was open to me was to press toward the edge of the wreck-pack, for there alone could I hope to find what I was after—and there it pretty certainly would be. But after my miserable experience of the preceding day it was plain that before I started on my hunting expedition I must hit upon some way of laying a course and holding it; or else, most likely, go rambling from wreck to wreck until I grew so weak from starvation that on one or another of them I should fall down at last and die.

Close beside me, as I sat on the hatch, was the brig's binnacle, and in it I could see the shrivelled remnant of what had been the compass-card; and the sight of this put into my head presently the thought—that might have got there sooner had

THIRST QUENCHED—COMPASS FOUND

my wits been sharper—to look for a compass still in working order and by means of it to steer some sort of a steady course. The argument against this plan was plain enough, and it was a strong one: that in holding as well as I could to any straight line I might only get deeper and deeper into my maze—for I was turned around completely, and while I knew that I could not be very far from the edge of my island of flotsam I had not the faintest notion in which direction that near edge lay.

For some minutes longer I sat on the hatch thinking the matter over and trying to hit on something that would open to me a better prospect of success; and all the while I had a hungry pain in my stomach that made clear thinking difficult, and that at the same time urged me to do quickly anything that gave even the least promise of getting food. And so the upshot of the matter was that I slung my two bottles of water over my shoulders with a bit of line that I found in the brig's cabin—making the slings short, that the bottles might hang close under my arms and be pretty safe against breaking—and then away I went on my cruise after a compass still on speaking terms with the north pole.

That I would find one seemed for a good while unlikely; for I searched a score and more of wrecks, and on every one of them the binnacle either was

IN THE SARGASSO SEA

empty or the needle entirely rusted away. But at last I came to a barque that had a newer look about her than that of the craft amidst which she was lying, and that also had her binnacle covered with a tarred canvas hood such as is used when vessels are lying in port. How the hood came to be where it was on that broken wreck was more than I could account for; but by reason of its being in place the binnacle had been well protected from the weather, and I found to my delight that the compass inside was in working trim.

It was an awkward thing to carry, being an old-fashioned big square box heavily and clumsily made; but I was so glad to get it that I was not for quarrelling with it, though it did for a little put me to a puzzle as to how I should pack it along. What I came to was to sling it on my back knapsack-fashion, which was a poor way to have it, since every time that I looked at it I had to unsling it and then to sling it again; yet there was no other way for me to manage it, because in my scrambling from one wreck to another I needs must have both hands free. But what with this big box strapped to my shoulders, and the two big bottles dangling close up under my arm-pits, I must have looked—only there was nobody to look at me—nothing less than a figure of fun.

As I knew not which way I ought to go, and so had all ways open to me, I laid my course for the

THIRST QUENCHED—COMPASS FOUND

head of the compass; and was the more disposed thus to go due north because that way, as far as I could see for the mist and the mast-tangle, the wrecks lay packed so close together that passing from one to another would be easy for me—which was a matter to be considered in view of the load that I had to carry along.

But just as I was ready to start another notion struck me. I had noticed the modern look of the barque, as compared with the ancient build of the hulks amidst which she was lying, when I first came aboard of her; and as I was about to leave her—my eye being caught by the soundness of a bit of line made fast to a belaying-pin on her rail—the thought occurred to me that I might find on her something or other still fit to be called food. And when this thought came to me I unslung my compass and my water-bottles in a hurry—for I was as ravenous as a man well could be.

XXII

I GET SOME FOOD IN ME AND FORM A CRAZY PLAN

The sun by that time being risen so high that the mist was changing again to a golden haze, and the cabin of the barque well lighted through the skylight over it, I felt less creepy and uncomfortable as I went down the companion-way than I had felt when I went below into the old brig's dusky cabin in the early dawn. But for all that I walked gingerly, and stopped to sniff at every step that I took downward; for I could not by any means get rid of my dread of coming upon some grewsome thing. However, the air was sweet enough—the slide of the hatch being closed, but the doors open and the cabin well ventilated—and when I got to the foot of the stair I saw nothing horrible in my first sharp look around.

It was a small cabin, but comfortably fitted; and almost the first thing that caught my eye was a work-basket spilled down into a corner and some spools and a pair of rusty scissors lying on the floor, and then in another corner I saw a little chair. And the sight of these things, which told

I GET FOOD AND FORM A PLAN

that the barque's captain had had his wife and his child along with him, gave me a heavy sorrowful feeling—for all that if death had come to this sea-family the pain of it must have been over quickly a long while back in the past.

Two of the state-room doors, both on the starboard side, were open; and both rooms were empty, save for the mouldy bedding in the bunks and in one of them a canvas bed-bag such as seamen use. The doors of the other two rooms, there being four in all, were closed, and I opened them hesitatingly; and felt a good deal easier in my mind when I found that in neither of them was what I dreaded might be there. In one of them the bunk had been left in disorder, as though some one had risen from it hurriedly, and a frock and a bonnet were hanging against the wall; but the other one seemed to have been used only as a sort of storeroom—there being in it a pair of rubber boots and a suit of oil-skins, and a locker in which were some pretty trifles in shell-work such as might have been picked up in a West Indian port, and a little rack of books gone mouldy with the damp. One of these books I opened, and found written on the flyleaf: "Mary Woodbridge, with Aunt Jane's love. For the coming Christmas of 1879"—and this date, though it did not settle certainly when the barque had started on the voyage that had come to so bad an ending, at least proved that she had not been lying where I found her for a very great many years.

As to how the barque had got so deep into the wreck-pack, she being so lately added to it, I could not determine; but my conjecture was that some storm had broken the pack and had driven her down into it, and then that the opening had closed again, leaving her fast a good way in its inside. But about the way of her getting there I did not much bother myself, my one strong thought being that I had a chance of finding on board of her something that I could eat; and so—being by that time pretty well satisfied that I was safe not to come upon anything horrid hid away in a dark corner of her—I went at my farther explorations with a will. Indeed, I was so desperately hungry by that time that even had I made some nasty discoveries I doubt if they would have held me back from my eager search for food.

Luckily I had not far to look before I found what I was after, the very first door that I tried— a door in the forward side of the cabin—opening into a pantry in which were stowed what had been, as I judged from the nature of them and the place where I found them, the captain's private stores. The door was not locked, and a good many empty boxes were lying around on the floor with splintered lids, as though they had been smashed open in a hurry—which looked as though the pantry had

I GET FOOD AND FORM A PLAN

been levied on suddenly to provision the boats after the wreck occurred, and so made me hope that the captain and his wife and baby had got away from the barque alive.

But the stock of stores had been a big one, and I saw that I was safe enough against starvation if only a part of what was left still were sound—and that uncertainty I settled in no time by picking up a hatchet that was lying among the broken boxes and splitting open the first tin on which I laid my hands. The tin had beans in it, and when I cracked it open that way more than half of them went flying over the floor; and they looked so good, those blessed beans, that without stopping to smell at them critically, or otherwise to test their soundness, I fell to feeding myself out of the open tin with my hand—and never stopped until all that remained of them were in my inside. I don't suppose that they were the better for having lain there so long, but they certainly were not much the worse for it—as I proved more conclusively, having by that time taken off the sharp edge of my hunger, by eating a part of another tin of them and finding them very good indeed. After that I opened a tin of meat—but on the instant that the hatchet split into it there came bouncing out such a dreadful smell that I had to rush on deck in a hurry with it and heave it over the side.

But even without the meat my food supply was

IN THE SARGASSO SEA

secure to me for a good while onward, there being no less than ten boxes with two dozen tins of beans in each of them—quite enough to keep life in me for more than half a year. I rummaged through the place thoroughly, but found nothing more that was fit to eat there. Some boxes of biscuit and a barrel of flour had gone musty until they fairly were rotten; and all the other things that I came across were spoiled utterly by damp and mould. As for the stores for the crew, when I went forward to have a look at them, they were spoiled too—the flour and biscuit rotten, and the pickled meat a mouldy mass of tough fibre encrusted thickly with salt.

One other thing I did find in the captain's pantry that was as good, save for the mould that coated the outside of it, as when it came aboard—and because of its excellent condition was all the more tantalizing. This was a case of plug tobacco—a bit of which shredded and filled into one of the pipes that I found with it, could I have got it lighted, would have made me for the moment almost a happy man. But as I could think of no way of lighting it I was worse off than if I had not found it at all.

Having made my tour of inspection and taken a general inventory of my new possessions, I came on deck again and seated myself on the roof of the cabin that I might do some quiet thinking about

I GET FOOD AND FORM A PLAN

what should be my next move; for I realized that only by a stroke of rare good fortune had I come upon this supply of food far away from the coast of my continent, and that should I leave it and keep on the course northward that I had set for myself I very likely might starve before another such store fell in my way. And yet, on the other hand, to stay on where I was merely because I was able to keep alive there—with no outlook of hope to stay me—was but making a bid for that madness which comes of despair.

As to carrying any great quantity of food on with me, it was a sheer impossibility. The tins of beans weighed each of them more than five pounds, and a score of them would make as much of a load as I well could carry on level ground—and far more of a load than I could manage in the scramble that was before me if I decided to go on. Indeed, I had found my two bottles of water a serious inconvenience; and yet I would have them to carry also, and the big compass too. As to water, however, since the shower of the morning, I felt less anxiety: and the event proved that my confidence in the rainfall was justified—for the showers came regularly a little after dawn, and only once or twice after that first sharp experience did I feel more than passing pain from thirst.

I sat there on the roof of the cabin for a good part of the morning cogitating the matter; and in the end I could think of no better plan than one which promised certainly a world of hard labor, and only promised uncertainly to serve my turn. This was to stick to my project of going steadily northward—carrying with me as much food as I could stagger under—until I came again to the outer edge of the wreck-pack; but to safeguard my return to the barque, should my food give out before my journey was accomplished, by blazing my path: that is to say, by making a mark on each wreck that I crossed so that I could retrace my steps easily and without fear of losing my way.

What I would gain in the end I did not try very clearly to tell myself—having only a vague feeling that in getting again to the coast of my great dead continent I would be that much the nearer to the living world once more; and having a clearer feeling that only by sticking at some sort of hard work that had a little hopefulness in it could I save myself from going mad. And I cannot but think now, looking back at it, that a touch of madness already was upon me; for no man ever set himself to a crazier undertaking than that to which I set myself then.

XXIII

HOW I STARTED ON A JOURNEY DUE NORTH

The morning was well spent by the time that I had made my mind up, and I was growing hungry again. I made a good meal on what was left in the second tin of beans that I had opened for my breakfast; and when I was done I tried to get a light for my pipe by rubbing bits of wood together, but made nothing of it at all. I had read about castaways on desert islands getting fire that way—but they went at it with dry wood, I fancy, and in my mist-sodden desert all the wood was soaked with damp.

For that afternoon I decided to go forward only as far as I could fetch it to be back on board the barque again by sunset, taking with me as many tins of beans as I could carry and leaving them where I made my turn: by which arrangement I would save the carriage of my supper and my breakfast, and would have a little store of victuals to fall back upon—when I should be fairly started on my journey—without coming all the way again to the barque.

IN THE SARGASSO SEA

I got the bed-bag that I had seen in the stateroom, and managed with the rusty scissors to cut it down to half its size. Into this I packed ten tins of beans, and made them snug by whipping around the bag one end of a longish line—which served when coiled as a handle for it; and, being uncoiled, enabled me to haul it up a ship's side after me, or to let it down ahead of me, or to sway it across an open space between two vessels, and so go at my climbing and jumping with both hands free. As for the compass, my back was the only place for it and I put it there—where it did not bother me much, having little weight; and I stuck the hatchet to blaze my path with into a sort of a belt that I made for myself with a bit of line.

Considering what a load I was carrying, and that on every vessel which I crossed I had to stop while I blazed a mark on her, I made a good long march of it before the waning of the daylight was a sign to me that I must put about again; and my return journey was both quick and easy, for I left the whole of my load, excepting the empty bag, behind me and came back lightly along my plainly marked path. But I was tired enough when I got on board the barque again, and glad enough to eat my supper and then stretch myself out to sleep upon the cabin floor.

That night, being easy in my body—except for my wholesome weariness—and easier in my mind because it seemed to me that I was doing something for my deliverance, and being also aboard a vessel that I knew was clean and pure, I had no visions of any kind whatever, but went to sleep almost in a moment, and slept like a log, as the saying is, the whole night through. Indeed, I slept later than suited my purposes — being for rising early and making a long day's march of it — and I might have wasted still more time in drowsing lazily had I not been wakened a little before sunrise by the rattle on the cabin roof of a dashing burst of rain. I was on deck in a moment, and by stopping a scupper — as I had done the previous morning — presently had by me a far bigger supply of water than I needed; from which I got a good drink lying down to it, and filled an empty bean-tin for another drink after my breakfast, and so had my two bottles full to last me until the next day — and was pretty well satisfied by the rain's recurrence that I could count upon a shower every morning about the hour of dawn.

When I had finished my breakfast I stowed ten tins of beans in the bag and lashed four more together so that I could carry them on my shoulders — being able to manage them in that way because I had no other back-load — and so was ready to set out along my blazed path. But before leaving the barque — hoping never again to lay eyes on her — I took one more look through the cabin to make sure that I had not passed over something that might be useful to me: and was lucky enough to find under one of the bunks a drawer—that had been hidden by the tumbled sheets hanging down over it—in which were some shirts and a suit of linen clothing that most opportunely supplied my needs. They all were badly mildewed, but sound enough, and the trousers—I had no use for the coat and waistcoat—fitted me very well. So I threw off the rags and tatters that I was wearing and put on in their place these sound garments; and then I picked up my load and was off.

Not having to stop to take bearings or to blaze my way, I made such good time that I got to the end of the course over which I had spent a good part of the previous afternoon in not much more than three hours. I was pretty well pleased to find that I could make such brisk marching under such a load; for it showed me that even when I should get a long way from my base of supplies, that is to say from the barque, I still could return to it at no great expense of time—and the thought never entered my head that time was of no value to me, since only by what would be close upon a miracle could I hope for anything better than to find ways for killing it through all the remainder of my days.

Being thus come to my place of deposit I had to rearrange my packing—going forward with a lighter load of food that I might carry also the compass and the hatchet; and going slowly because of my constant stops to take fresh bearings and to mark my path. But that time I went straight onward until nightfall; and my heart sank a good deal within me as I found that the farther I went the more antique in model, and the more anciently sea-worn, were the wrecks which I came upon—and so I knew that I must be making my way steadily into the very depths of my maze.

Yet I could not see that I would gain anything by going back to the barque and thence taking a fresh departure. The barque, as I knew certainly from the sort of craft surrounding her, was so deeply bedded in the pack that no matter how I headed from her I should have to go far before I came again to the coast of it; and on the other hand I thought that by holding to my course northward I might work my way in no great time across the innermost huddle of ancient wrecks—for of the vast number of these I had no notion then—and so to the outer belt of wrecks new-made: on board of which I certainly should find fresh food in plenty, and from which (as I forced myself to believe) I might get away once more into the living world. And so I pushed on doggedly until the twilight changed to dusk and I could not venture farther; and then I ate my supper on board of a strange old ship, as round as a dumpling and with a high bow and a higher stern; and when I had finished settled myself for the night, being very weary, under the inhang of her heavy bulging side.

When morning came—and a shower with it that gave me what drink I wanted and a store of water for the day—I debated for a while with myself as to whether I should go onward with my whole load, or leave a part of it in a fresh deposit to which I could return at will. The second course seemed the better to me; and, indeed, it was necessary for me to go light-loaded in order to get on at all. For I had come among ships of such strange old-fashioned build, standing at bow and stern so high out of the water, that unless they happened to be lying side by side so that I could pass from one to another amidships—which was the case but seldom—I had almost as much climbing up and down among them as though I had been a monkey mounting and descending a row of trees.

Therefore I ate as much breakfast as I could pack into myself—that being as good a way as any other of carrying food with me—and then I tore the sleeves from my shirt and stuffed them from the tins that I opened until I had two great bean sausages, which I fastened belt-fashion about my waist and so carried without any trouble at all. Indeed, but for this new arrangement of my load I doubt if I could have gone onward; and even with it I

HOW I STARTED DUE NORTH

had all that I could do to make my way. The bag with the remaining tins in it I stood away inside the cabin of the old ship—which I should have explored farther, so strange-looking was it, but for my eager desire to get on; and I felt quite sure that I would find all just as I had left it there even though I did not come back again for twenty years.

XXIV

OF WHAT I FOUND ABOARD A SPANISH GALLEON

BENT as I was upon hurrying forward, I could not but stop often in my wearying marches—which began each morning at sunrise and did not end until dusk—to gaze about me in wonder at the curious ancient craft across which lay my way. It seemed to me, indeed, as though I had got into a great marine museum where were stored together all manner of such antique vessels as not for two full centuries, and a good many of them for still longer, had sailed the seas. Some of them were mere shallops, so little that sailormen nowadays would not venture to go a-coasting in them, and others were great round-bellied old merchantmen—yet half war-ships, too—with high-built fore-castles, and towering poops blossoming out into rich carvings and having galleries rising one above another and with a big iron lantern at the top of all. And all of them had been shattered in fights and tempests, and were so rotten with age that the decks beneath my feet were soft and spongy; and all were weathered to a soft gray, or to a brownish

ABOARD A SPANISH GALLEON

blackness, with here and there a gleam of bright upon them where there still clung fast in some protected recess of their carving a little of the heavy gilding with which it all had been overlaid. Guns of some sort were on every one of them—ranging upward from little swivels mounted on the rail (mere pop-guns they looked like) to long bronze pieces of which the delicate ornamentation was lost in a thick coat of verdigris that had been gathering slowly through years and years. But as to the strange rig that they had worn in their days of active sea-faring, I could only guess at it; for such of them as had come into this death-haven with any of their top-hamper still standing, as some of them no doubt had come, long since had lost it—first the standing-rigging and later the masts rotting, and so all together falling in a heap anyway upon the decks or over the side. And such a company of withered old sea-corpses as these ancient wrecks made there, all huddled together with the weed thick about them, was as hopeless and as dismal a sight as ever was seen by the eyes of man.

But a matter that to me was more instantly dismal, as I pressed on among them, came when I found that I was getting so close to the end of my stock of provisions—while yet apparently no nearer to the end of my journey—that there was no shirking the necessity of returning to the distant barque for a fresh supply: a journey involving such desperate toil, and so much of it, that the mere thought of it sent aches through all my bones.

It was about noon one day, while I was trying to nerve myself to make this hard expedition, that I called a halt in order to eat my dinner—which I knew would be a very little one—being just then come aboard of a great ungainly galleon that from the look of her I thought could not be less than two centuries and a half old: she being more curiously ancient in her build than any vessel that I had got upon, and her timbers so rotten that I had ticklish climbing as I worked my way up her high quarter—and, indeed, one of her galleries giving way under me, was near to spilling down her tall side to my death beneath the tangled weed. And when at last I got to her deck I found it so soft, partly with rottenness and partly with a sort of moss growing over it, that I was fearful at each step that it would give way under me and let me down with a crash into her hold.

I would have been glad of a better place to eat my dinner in—she being sodden wet everywhere, and with a chill about her for all the warmth of the misty air shimmering with dull sunshine, and with a rank unwholesome smell rising from her rotting mass. But all the hulks thereabouts were in so much the same condition that by going on I was not likely greatly to better myself; and I was so tired and so hungry that I had no heart to attempt any more hard scrambling until I had had both rest and food. And so I hunted out a spot on her deck where the moss was thinnest and least oozy with moisture—being a place a little sheltered by a sort of porch above her cabin doorway—and there I seated myself and with a good deal of satisfaction fell to upon my very scanty ration of beans.

For a while I was busied wholly with my eating, being mighty sharp set after my morning's walk; but when my short meal was ended I began to look about me, and especially to peer into the deep old cabin—that was pretty well lighted through the stern-windows and through the doorway at my shoulder, of which the door had rotted away.

From where I was seated I could see nearly the whole of it; and what I first noted was that a little hatch in the middle of the floor was open, and that dangling down into it from one of the roof-beams was a double-purchase—as though an attempt to haul up some heavy thing from that place had come to a short end. For the rest, there was little to see: only a clumsy table set fast between fixed benches close under the stern windows; a locker in which I found, when I looked into it, a sodden thing that very likely had been the ship's log-book along with a queer old Jacob's staff (as they were called) such as mariners took their observations with before quadrants were known; and against the wall were hanging a couple of long old rusty swords and a rusty thing that I took at first to be a wash-basin, but made out was a deep-curved breast-plate that must have belonged to a very round-bellied little man.

The floor of the cabin, as I found when I went in there, was so firm and solid—being laid in teak, very likely, and having been sheltered by the roof over it from the rains—that I had no fear, as I had on the open deck, that the planks would give way under me and let me through. And when I was come inside I found resting on a wooden rack set against the front wall a couple of old bell-mouthed brass fire-locks, coated thick with verdigris, and with them three smaller bell-mouthed pieces which were neither guns nor pistols but something between the two. As for the log-book, if it were the log-book, I could make nothing of it. It was so soaked and swelled by the dampness, and so rotten, that my fingers sank into it when I tried to pick it up as they would have sunk into porridge; and the slimy stuff left a horrid smell upon my hand. Therefore I cannot tell what was the name of this old ship, nor to what country she belonged, nor whither she was sailing on her last voyage; but that she was Spanish—or perhaps Portuguese—and was wrecked while on her way homeward from some port in the Indies, I do not doubt at all.

When I had made my round of the cabin, finding so little, I came to the open hatch in the middle of it and gazed down into the dusky depth curiously: wondering a good deal that in what must have been almost the moment when death was setting its clutch upon the galleon, and when all aboard of her assuredly were in peril of their lives, her people should have tried to rouse out a part of her cargo—as I had proof that they had tried to do in the tackle still hanging there from the beam. And the only reasonable way to account for this strange endeavor, it seemed to me—since provisions were not likely to be carried in that part of the vessel—was that something so precious was down there in the blackness as to make the risk of death worth taking in order to try to save it from the sea.

With that there came over me an itching curiosity to find out what the treasure was which the crew of the galleon—in such stress of some sort that they had been forced to give up the job suddenly—had tried to get out of their ship and carry off with them; and along with my curiosity came an eager pounding of my heart as I thought to myself—without ever stopping to think also how useless riches of any sort were to me—that by right of discovery their treasure, whatever it might be, had become mine.

With my breath coming and going quickly, I got down upon my hands and knees and stooped my head well into the opening that I might get rid of the light in my eyes from the cabin windows; and being that way I made out dimly that the lower block of the purchase was whipped fast to a little wooden box, and that other small boxes were stowed in regular tiers under it so that they filled snugly a little chamber about a dozen feet square. That there were several layers of these boxes seemed probable, for those in sight were only six feet or so below the level of the cabin floor, and that they held either gold or silver I considered to be beyond a doubt; and as I raised my head up out of the hatch, my eyes blinking as the light struck them, and thought of the wealth that must be stored there in that little chamber, and that it was mine because I had found it, I gave a long great sigh.

For a minute or two I was quite dazed by my discovery; and then as I got steadier—or got crazier, perhaps I ought to say—nothing would serve me but that I must get down to where my treasure was, so that my eyes might see it and that I might touch it with my hands. And with that I caught at the tackle and gave a tug on the ropes to test them, and as they held I swung to them to slide down—and the moment that my full weight was on them they snapped like punk, and down I went feet foremost and struck on the tiers of boxes with a bang. As I fell only a little way, and upon a

ABOARD A SPANISH GALLEON

level surface—for I went clear of the box to which the tackle was made fast—no harm came to me; but under my feet I felt the rotten wood going squashily, and then beneath it something firm and hard. And when I got back my balance and looked down eagerly my eyes caught a dull gleam in the semi-darkness, and then made out beneath my feet a mass of yellow ingots: and I gave a great shout—that seemed to be forced out of me to keep my heart from bursting—for I knew that I was standing on bars of gold!

XXV

I AM THE MASTER OF A GREAT TREASURE

FOR a while, down in that black little place, I was quite a crazy creature; being so stirred by my finding this great store of riches that I went to dancing and singing there — and was not a bit bothered by the vile stench rising from the rotten wood that my feet sent flying, nor by the still viler stench rising from the reeking mass of rottenness below me in the galleon's hold.

And then, that I might see my treasure the more clearly, I fell to tossing the ingots up through the hatch into the cabin—where I could have a good light upon them, and could gloat upon the yellow gleam of them, and could make some sort of a guess at how much each of them represented in golden coin. From that I went on to calculating how much the whole of them were worth together; and when I got to the end of my figuring I fairly was dazed.

In a rough way I estimated that each ingot weighed at least five pounds, and as each of the little boxes contained ten of them the value of

I AM THE MASTER OF TREASURE

every single box stored there was not less than fifteen thousand dollars. As well as I could make out, the boxes were in rows of ten and there were ten rows of them—which gave over a million and a half of dollars for the top tier alone; and as there certainly was an under-tier the value of my treasure at the least was three millions. But actually, as I found by digging down through the ingots until I came to the solid flooring, there were in all five tiers of boxes; and what made the whole of them worth close upon eight millions of our American money, or well on toward two millions of English pounds. My brain reeled as I thought about it. The treasure that I had possession of was a fortune fit for a king!

I had swung myself up from the little chamber and was standing in the cabin while I made these calculations, and when at last I got to my sum total I felt so light-headed that it seemed as though I were walking on air. Indeed, I fairly was stunned by my tremendous good fortune and could not think clearly: and it was because my mind thus was turned all topsy-turvy, I suppose, that the odd thought popped into it that in the matter of weight my gold ingots were pretty much the same as the tins of beans to get which I was about to return to the barque—a foolish notion which so tickled my fancy that I burst out into a loud laugh.

The jarring sound of my laughter, which rang

out with a ghastly impropriety in that deathly place, brought me to my senses a little and made me calmer. But my mind ran on for a moment or so upon the odd notion that had provoked it, and in that time certain other thoughts flashed into my head which had only to get there to spill out of me every bit of my crazy joy. For first I realized that since I could carry only the same weight of gold that I could carry of food my actual wealth was but a single back-load, which brought my millions down to a few beggarly thousands; and on top of that I realized—and this came like a douse of ice-water—that for every ingot that I carried away with me I must leave a like weight of food behind: which meant neither more nor less than that my great treasure, for all the good that ever it would be to me—so little could I venture to take of it on these terms—might as well be already at the bottom of the sea.

And then, being utterly dispirited and broken, I fell to thinking how little difference it made one way or the other—how even a single ingot would be a vain lading—since I had no ground for hoping that ever again would I get to a region where I would have use for gold. And with that—though I kept on staring in a dull way at the ingots scattered over the floor of the cabin—I thought of the treasure no longer: my heart being filled with a great sorrowing pity for myself, because of the doom upon me to live out whatever life might be left me in the most horrid solitude into which ever a man was cast.

For a long while I stood despairing there; and then at last the hope of life began to rise in me again—as it always must rise, no matter how desperate are the odds against it, in the mind of a sound and vigorous man. And with this saner feeling came again my desire to push on in the direction that offered me a chance of deliverance— leaving all my treasure behind me, since it was worth less to me than food; and presently came the farther hope that when I had succeeded in finding a way out of my sea-prison, and so was sure of my life once more, I might be able to return to the galleon and take away with me at least some portion of the great riches that I had found.

Because of this foolish hope, and the very human comfort that I found in knowing myself to be the possessor of such prodigious wealth, I needs must jump down again to where it was and take another survey of it before I left it behind. And then, being cooler and looking more carefully, I noticed that the box to which the tackle had been made fast was not like the other boxes—though about the same size with them—but was a little coffer that seemed once to have been locked and that still had around it the rusty remnants of iron bands. This difference in the make of it put into my head the notion that its contents were more precious than the contents of the other boxes—though how that could be I did not well see; and my notion seemed the more reasonable as I reflected that if the coffer really were of an extraordinary value there would have been sense in trying to save it even in a time of great peril—which was more than could be said of trying to load down boats launched in the midst of some final disaster with any of those heavy boxes of gold.

My mind became excited by another mirage of riches as these thoughts went through it, and to settle the matter I stooped down and got a grip on the coffer—which was made of a tougher wood than the boxes and held together—and managed by a good deal of straining to lift it up through the hatch into the cabin, where I could examine it at my ease.

When it was new an axe would not have made much impression upon it, so strongly had it been put together; but there were left only black stains to show where the iron had bound it, and the wood had rotted until it was softer than the softest bit of pine. Indeed, I had only to give a little jerk to the lid to open it: both the lock and the hinges being gone with rust, and the lid held in place only by a sort of sticky slime.

But when I did get it open the first thing that came out of it was a stench so vile that I had to

I AM THE MASTER OF TREASURE

jump up in a hurry and rush to the open deck until the worst of it had ebbed away; and this exceeding evil odor was given off by a slimy ooze of rotted leather—as I knew a little later by finding still unmelted some bits of small leather bags in which what was stored there had been tied. But even as I jumped up and left the cabin my eyes caught a gleam of brightness in the horrid slimy mess that set my heart to beating hard again; and it pounded away in my breast still harder when I came back and made out clearly what I had found.

For there in the rotten ooze, strewn thickly, was such a collection of glittering jewels that my eyes fairly were dazzled by them; and when I had turned the coffer upside down on the deck so that the slime flowed away stickily—giving off the most dreadful stench that ever I have encountered—I saw a heap of precious stones such as for size and beauty has not been gathered into one place, I suppose—unless it may have been in the treasury of some Eastern sovereign—since the very beginning of the world. At a single glance I knew that the great treasure of gold, which had seemed to me overwhelming because of its immensity, was as nothing in comparison with this other treasure wherein riches were so concentrate and sublimate that I had the very essence of them: and I reeled and trembled again as I hugged the thought to me that by my finding of it I was made master of it all.

XXVI

OF A STRANGE SIGHT THAT I SAW IN THE NIGHT-TIME

I WAS pretty much mooning mad for a while, I suppose: sometimes walking about the cabin and thrusting with my feet contemptuously at the gold ingots strewn over the floor of it, and sometimes standing still in a sort of rapt wonder over my heap of jewels—and anything like sensible thinking was quite beyond the power of my unbalanced mind. But at last I was aroused, and so brought to myself a little, by the daylight waning suddenly: as it did in that region when the sun dropped down into the thick layer of mist lying close upon the water—making at first a strange purplish dusk, and then a rich crimson after-glow that deepened into purple again, and so turning slowly into blackness as night came on.

When I had come aboard the galleon, about noon-time, and had found her so sodden with wet and so reeking with foul odors—as, indeed, were all of the very ancient ships which made the mid-part of that sea graveyard—I had made my mind up to a forced march in the afternoon that I hoped would carry me through the worst of all that rottenness, and so to a ship partly dry and less ill-smelling for the night. But when I came out from the cabin and looked about me, and saw how thick and black were the shadows in the clefts between the wrecks, I knew that I could not venture onward, but must pass the night where I was. And this was a prospect not at all to my mind.

The cabin, of course, was the only place for me, the soaked deck with the soaked moss on top of it being quite out of the question; but even the cabin was not fit for a dog to lie in, so chill and damp was it and so foul with the stench rising and spreading from the slime of rotted leather that I had emptied from the coffer and that made a little vile pool upon the floor. And through the open hatch there came up a dismal heavy odor of all the rotten stuff down there that almost turned my stomach, and that made the air laden with it hard to breathe —though in my hot excitement I had not noticed it at all. But this last I got the better of in part by covering again the opening, though I had to move the hatch very gently and carefully to keep it from falling into rotten fragments in my hands. Yet because it was so dense with moisture, when I did get it set in place, it pretty well kept the stench down. And then I kicked away some of the ingots into a corner, and so cleared a space on the floor where I could stretch myself just within the cabin door.

These matters being attended to, I seated myself in the same place where I had eaten my dinner—just outside the door, under the little sort of porch overhanging it—and ate the short ration that I allowed myself for my supper, and found it very much less than my lively hunger required. When I had finished I sat on there for a good while longer, being very loath to go into the cabin; but at last, by finding myself nodding with weary drowsiness, I knew that sleep would come quickly, and so went inside and laid myself down upon the floor. There still was a faint glimmer of dying daylight outside, and this little glow somehow comforted me as I lay there facing the doorway and blinking now and then before my eyes were tight closed; but I did not lie long that way half-waking, being so utterly fagged in both mind and body that I dropped off into deep slumber before the darkness fell.

I suppose that even in my sleep I had an uneasy sense of my bleak surroundings; and that this, in the course of three or four hours—by which time I was a good deal rested and so slept less soundly—got the better of my weariness and roused me awake again. But when I first woke I was sure that I had slept the night through and that early morning was come—for there was so much light in the cabin that I never thought to account for it save by the return of day. Yet the light was not like daylight, as I realized when I had a little more shaken off my sleepiness, being curiously white and soft.

I turned over—for I had rolled in my uneasy sleep and got my back toward the doorway—and raised myself a little on my elbow so that I might see out clearly; and what I saw was so unearthly strange, and in a way so awe-compelling, that in another moment I was on my feet and staring with all my eyes. Over the whole deck of the galleon a soft lambent light was playing, and this went along her bulwarks and up over her high fore-castle so that all the lines of her structure were defined sharply by it; and pale through the mist against the blackness, out over her low waist, I could catch glimpses of the other tall old ships lying near her all likewise shining everywhere with the same soft flames—which yet were not flames exactly, but rather a flickering glow.

In a moment or so I realized that this luminous wonder, which at the first look had so strong a touch of the supernatural in it, was' no more than the manifestation of a natural phenomenon: being the shimmer of phosphorescent light upon the soaking rotten woodwork of the galleon and of the ships about her, as rotten and as old. But making this explanation to myself did not lessen the frightening strangeness of the spectacle, nor do much to stop the cold creeps which ran over me as I looked at it: I being there solitary in that marvellous brightness—that I knew was in a way a death-glow—the one thing alive.

But presently my unreasoning shivering dread began to yield a little, as my curiosity bred in me an eager desire to see the whole of this wondrous soft splendor; for I made sure from my glimpses over the galleon's bulwarks that it was about me on every side. And so I stepped out from the cabin upon the deck, where my feet sank into the short mossy growth that coated the rotten planks and I was fairly walking in what seemed like a lake of wavering pale flame; and from there, that I might see the better, I climbed cautiously up the rotten stair leading to the roof of the cabin, and thence to the little over-topping gallery where the stern-lantern was. And from that height I could gaze about me as far as ever the mist would let me see.

Everywhere within the circle that my eyes covered—which was not a very big one, for in the night the mist was thick and low-lying—the old wrecks wedged together there were lighted with the same lambent flames: which came and went over their dead carcasses as though they all suddenly were lighted and then as suddenly were put out again; and farther away the glow of them in the mist was like a silvery shimmering haze.

STRANGE SIGHT IN THE NIGHT-TIME

By this ebbing and flowing light—which seemed to me, for all that I knew the natural cause of it, so outside of nature that I thrilled with a creeping fear as I looked at it—I could see clearly the shapes of the strange ancient ships around me: their great poops and fore-castles rising high above their shallow waists, and here and there among them the remnant of a mast making a line of light rising higher still—like a huge corpse-candle shining against the blackness beyond. And the ruin of them—the breaks in their lines, and the black gaps where bits of their frames had rotted away completely—gave to them all a ghastly death-like look; while their wild tangling together made strange ragged lines of brightness wavering under the veil of mist, as though a desolate sea-city were lying there dead before me lit up with lanterns of despair.

Yet that which most keenly thrilled me with a cold dread was my strong conviction that I could see living men moving hither and thither over those pale-lit decks, where my reason told me that only ancient death could be; for the play of the flickering light made such a commotion of fleeting flames and dancing shadows, going and coming in all manner of fantastic shapes, that every shattered hulk around me seemed to have her old crew alive and on board of her again—all hurrying in bustling crowds fore and aft, and up and down the heights of her, as though under orderly command.

IN THE SARGASSO SEA

And at times these shapes were so real and so distinct to me that I was for crying out to them—and would check myself suddenly, shivering with a fright which I knew was out of all reason but which for the life of me I could not keep down.

And so the night wore away: while I stood there on the galleon's poop with the soft pale flames flickering around me in the mist, and my fears rising and falling as I lost and regained control of myself; and I think that it is a wonder that I did not go mad.

XXVII

I SET MYSELF TO A HEAVY TASK

At last, after what seemed to me an age of waiting for it, a little pinkish tone began to glow in the mist to the eastward; and as that honest light got stronger the death-fires on the old galleon and on the wrecks around her paled quickly until they were snuffed out altogether—and then came the customary morning down-pour of rain.

With the return of the blessed daylight, and with the enlivening douse of cool fresh water upon me, I got to be myself again: my fanciful fears of the night-time leaving me, and my mind coming back soberly to a consideration of my actual needs. Of these the most pressing, as my stomach told me, was to get my breakfast; and when that matter, in a very poor way, had been attended to, and I had drunk what water I needed—without much relishing it—from a pool that had formed on the deck where the timbers sagged down a little, I was in better heart to lay out for myself a plan of campaign.

In one way planning was not necessary. By

holding to a northerly course I believed that I had got at least half way across my continent, and my determination was fixed to keep on by the north—rather than risk a fresh departure that might only carry me by a fresh way again into the depths of the tangle—until I should come once more to the open sea: if I may call open sea that far outlying expanse of ocean covered with thick-grown weed. But it was needful that I should plan for my supply of food as I went onward, that was to be got only by returning to the far-away barque; and also I felt an itching desire—as strong as at first blush it was unreasonable—to carry away with me some part of the treasure that I had found. That I ever should get out into the world again, and so have the good of my riches, seemed likely to me only in my most sanguine moments; but even on the slimmest chance of accomplishing my own deliverance I had a very natural human objection to leaving behind me the wealth that I had found through such peril—only to lie there for a while longer idly, and then to be lost forever when the galleon sank to the bottom of the sea.

As to the gold, it was plain that I could carry off so little of it that I might as well resign myself—having that which was better worth working for—to losing it all. But my treasure of jewels was another matter. This was so very much more valuable than the gold—for the stones for the most

I SET MYSELF TO A HEAVY TASK

part were of a prodigious size and a rare fineness—that between the two there really was no comparison; and at the same time it was so compact in bulk and so petty in weight that I might easily carry the whole of it with me and a good store of food too. And so, to make a beginning, I picked the stones out of the slimy and stinking ooze in which they were lying and washed them clean in the pool of water on the deck; and then I packed them snugly into the shirt-sleeve in which my beans had been stored—and tickled myself the while with the fancy that most men would be willing for the sake of stuffing a shirt-sleeve that way to cut off the arm to which it belonged.

My packing being finished, and my precious bag laid away in a corner of the cabin until I should come to fetch it again, I was in a better mood for facing my long march back to the barque: for I had come to have fortune as well as life to work for, and those two strong stimulants to endeavor working together gave my spirits a great upward pull. And, fortunately, my cheerfulness staid by me through my long scrambling struggle backward along my blazed path; nor was it, in reality, as hard a journey as I had expected it to be—for I had but a light load of food to carry, barely enough to last me through, and the marks which I had left upon the wrecks in passing made my way plain. And so, at last, I got back to the barque one evening about sunset, and had almost a feeling of homecoming in boarding her again; and I was thankful enough to be able to eat all the supper I wanted, and then to lie down comfortably in her clean cabin and to rest myself in sound slumber after my many restless nights on rotten old ships reeking with a chill dampness that struck into my very bones.

I slept soundly and woke refreshed; and for that I was thankful, since the work cut out for me—to get back to the galleon with enough provisions to last me until I could cross the rest of the wreck-pack—was about as much as a strong man in good condition could do. However, I had thought of something that would make this hard job less difficult; for the ease with which I had carried a part of my food in long narrow bags, sausage-fashion—thereby getting rid of both the weight and the awkwardness of the tins—had put into my head the notion of carrying in that way the whole of my fresh supply, and so carrying at least twice as much of it. And I calculated—since I could go rapidly along my blazed path—that by cutting myself down to very short rations I could get back to the galleon with a bigger stock of provisions than that with which I left the barque when I made my first start toward the north—and if the galleon lay, as I believed that she did, about in the centre of the pack, this would give me enough food to last me until I got across to the other side.

I SET MYSELF TO A HEAVY TASK

So I rummaged out some more of the linen shirts that I had found—taking a fresh one for my own wear to begin with—and set myself to my sausage-making with the sleeves of them; packing each sleeve with beans as tight as I could ram it, and working over each a netting of light line that I finished off with loops at the ends. Ten of my big sausages I made into a bundle to be carried on my shoulders like a knapsack; and the rest I arranged to swing by their loops from a rope collar about my neck, with another rope run through the lower loops to be made fast about my waist and so hold them steady—and this arrangement, as I found when I tried it, answered very well. And finally, that I might carry my jewels the more securely, I cut off a sleeve from the oil-skin jacket to serve for an outer casing for them, and took along also some of the light line to net over the bundle and make it solid and strong; in that way guarding against the chance of their rubbing a hole in their linen covering—by which I might have lost them all.

I worked fast over my packing, and got it all finished and was ready to start away by not a great while after sunrise; yet when the time for my start came I hesitated a little, so darkly uncertain seemed the issue of the adventure that I had in hand. Indeed, the whole of my project was a wild one, such as no man not fairly driven into it would have entertained at all. Its one certainty was that only by excessive toil could I even hope to carry it through. All else was doubtful: for I knew not how distant were the farther bounds of the desolate dead region into which I was bent upon penetrating; nor had I ground for believing —since I had food in plenty where I was—that I would gain anything by traversing it; and back of all that was the gloomy chance of some accident befalling me that would end in my dying miserably by the way. While I was busily employed in making ready for my march I had grown quite cheerful; but suddenly my little crop of good spirits withered within me, and when at last I did go forward it was with a very heavy heart.

XXVIII

HOW I RUBBED SHOULDERS WITH DESPAIR

COULD I have foreseen all that was ahead of me I doubt if I should have had the courage to go on: choosing rather to stay there on the barque until I had eaten what food I had by me, and then to die slowly—and finding that way easier than the one I chose to follow, with its many days of struggle and its many chill nights of sorrow and I throughout the whole of it rubbing shoulders with despair.

As I think of it now, that long, long march seems to me like a horrible nightmare; and sometimes it comes back to me as a real nightmare in my dreams. Again, always heavy laden, I am climbing and scrambling and jumping, endlessly and hopelessly, among old rotten hulks; each morning trying to comfort myself with the belief that by night I may see some sign of ships less ancient, and so know that I am winning my way a little toward where I would be; and each night finding myself still surrounded by tall antique craft such as have not for two centuries and more held the seas, with the feeling coming down crushingly upon me that I have not advanced at all; and even then no good rest for me—as I lie down wearily in some foul-smelling old cabin, chill with heavy night-mist and with the reeking damp of oozy rotten timbers, and perhaps find in it for my sleeping-mates little heaps of fungus outgrowing from dead men's bones. And the mere dream of all this so bitterly hurts me that I wonder how I ever came through the reality of it alive.

At the start, as I have said, I had calculated that the treasure-laden galleon lay about in the centre of the wreck-pack, and therefore that I would get across from her to the other side of the pack in about the same time that I had taken to reach her in my first journey from the barque; and on the basis of that assumption, when I was come to her again, I shaped my course hopefully for the north. But my calculation, though on its face a reasonable enough one, proved to be most wofully wrong: and I have come to the conclusion, after a good deal of thinking about it, that this was because the whole vast mass of wreckage had a circular motion—the great current that created it giving at the same time a swirl to it—which made the seemingly straight line that I followed in reality a constantly extended curve. But whatever the cause may have been, the fact remains that when by my calculation I should have been on the outer edge of the wreck-pack I still was wandering in its depths.

I RUB SHOULDERS WITH DESPAIR

In one way my march was easier the longer that it lasted, my load growing a little lighter daily as my store of food was transferred to my stomach from my back. At first this steady decrease of my burden was a comfort to me; but after a while—when more than half of it was gone, and I still seemed to be no nearer to the end of my journey than when I left the galleon—I had a very different feeling about it: for I realized that unless I came speedily to ships whereon I would find food—of which there seemed little probability, so ancient were the craft surrounding me—I either must go back to the barque and wait on her until death came to me slowly, or else die quickly where I was. And so I had for my comforting the option of a tardy death or a speedy one—with the certainty of the latter if I hesitated long in choosing between the two.

I suppose that the two great motive powers in the world are hope and despair. It was hope that started me on that dismal march, but if despair had not at last come in to help me I never should have got to its end: for I took Death by both shoulders and looked straight into the eyes of him when I decided, having by me only food for three days longer—and at that but as little as would keep the life in me—to give over all thought of returning to the barque and to make a dash forward as fast as I could go.

I had little enough to carry, but that I might have still less I left my hatchet behind me—having, indeed, no farther use for it since if my dash miscarried I was done for and there was no use in marking a path over which I never could return; and I was half-minded to leave my bag of jewels behind me too. But in the end I decided to carry the jewels along with me—my fancy being caught by the grim notion that if I did die miserably in that vile solitude at least I would die one of the richest men in all the world. As to my water-bottles, one of them I had thrown away when I found that I could count on the morning showers certainly, and the other had been broken in one of my many tumbles: yet without much troubling me—as I found that I could manage fairly well, eating but little, if I filled myself pretty full of water at the beginning of each day. And so, with only the bag of food and the bag of jewels upon my back, and with the compass on top of them, I was ready to press onward to try conclusions with despair.

The very hopelessness of my effort, and the fact that at last I was dealing with what in one way was a certainty—for I knew that if my plan miscarried I had only a very little while longer to live—gave me a sort of stolid recklessness which amazingly helped me: stimulating me to taking risks in climbing which before I should have shrunk

I RUB SHOULDERS WITH DESPAIR

from, and so getting me on faster; and at the same time dulling my mind to the dreads besetting it and my body to its ceaseless pains begot of weariness and thirst and scanty food. So little, indeed, did I care what became of me that even when by the middle of my second day's march I saw no change in my surroundings I did not mind it much: but, to be sure, at the outset of this last stage of my journey I had thrown hope overboard, and a man once become desperate can feel no farther ills.

But what does surprise me—as I think of it now, though it did not in any way touch me then—was the slowness with which, when there was reason for it, my dead hope got alive again: as it did, and for cause, at the end of that same second day—for by the evening I came out, with a sharp suddenness, from among the strange old craft which for so long on every side had beset me and found myself among ships which by comparison with the others—though they too, in all conscience, were old enough—seemed to be quite of a modern build. What is likely, I think—and this would help to account for my long wanderings over those ancient rotten hulks—is that some stormy commotion of the whole mass of wreckage, such as had thrust the barque whereon I had found food deep into the thick of it, had squeezed a part of the centre of the pack outward; in that way making a sort of promontory — along which by mere bad mischance I had been journeying—among the wrecks of a later time. But this notion did not then occur to me; nor did I, as I have said, at first feel any very thrilling hope coming back to me when I found myself among modern ships again—so worn had my long tussle with difficulties left my body and so sodden was my mind.

At first I had just a dull feeling of satisfaction that I had got once more—after my many nights passed on hulks soaked with wet to rottenness—on good honest dry planks: where I could sleep with no deadly chill striking into me, and where in my restless wakings I should not see the pale gleam of death-fires, and where foul stenches would not half stifle me the whole night long. And it was not until I had eaten my scant supper, and because of the comfort that even that little food gave me felt more disposed to cheerfulness, that in a weak faint-hearted way I began to hope again that perhaps the run of luck against me had come to an end.

In truth, though, there was not much to be hopeful about. For my supper I had eaten the half of what food was left me, and it was so little that I still had a mighty hungry feeling in my belly after it was down. For my breakfast I should eat what was left; and after that, unless I found fresh supplies quickly, I was in a fair way to lie down be-

I RUB SHOULDERS WITH DESPAIR

side my bag of jewels and die of starvation—like the veriest beggar that ever was. But I did hope a little all the same; and when I went on again the next morning, though my last scrap of food was eaten, my spirits kept up pretty well—for I was sure from the look of the wrecks which I traversed that the dead ancient centre of my continent at last was behind me, and that its living outer fringe could not be very far away.

All that day I pressed forward steadily, helped by my little flickering flame of hope—which burned low because sanguine expectation does not consort well with an empty stomach, yet which kept alive because the wreck-pack had more and more of a modern look about it as I went on. But the faintness that I felt coming over me as the day waned gave me warning that the rope by which I held my life was a short one; and as the sun dropped down into the mist—at once thinning it, so that I could see farther, and giving it a ruddy tone which sent red streams of brightness gleaming over the tangle of wreckage far down into the west—I felt that the rope must come to an end altogether, and that I must stop still and let death overtake me, by the sunset of one day more.

And then it was, just as the sun was sinking, that I saw clearly—far away to the westward—the funnel of a steamer standing out black and sharp against the blood-red ball that in another minute went down into the sea. And with that glimpse—which made me sure that I was close to the edge of the wreck-pack, and so close to food again—a strong warm rush of hope swept through me that outcast finally my despair.

XXIX

I GET INTO A SEA CHARNEL-HOUSE

THAT I should get to the steamer that night I knew was clean impossible, for she lay a long way off from me, and that I had seen her funnel at all was due to the mere happy accident of its standing for that single minute directly between me and the setting sun. I did hope, though, that by pressing hard toward her I might fetch aboard of some vessel not long wrecked on which I would find eatable food; yet in this I was disappointed, the shadows coming down on me so fast that I was forced in a little while to pull up short—stopping while still a little daylight remained so that I might stow myself the more comfortably for the night.

As to looking for provender on the little old ship that I settled to camp on, I knew that it was useless. From her build I fixed her as belonging to the beginning of the present century, and from her depth in the wreck-pack she probably had met her death-storm not less than threescore years before; and so what provisions she had carried long since had wasted away. Yet there was a chance that I might find some spirits aboard of her—which would be a poor substitute for food, but better than nothing—and I hurried to have a look in her cabin before darkness settled down.

The cabin hatch was closed, and as it was both locked and swelled with moisture I could not budge it; but two or three kicks sent the doors beneath the hatch flying and so opened an entrance for me—that I was slow to make use of because of a heavy musty stench which poured out from that shut up place and made me turn a little sick, as I got my first strong whiff of it. Indeed, I was so faint and so hungry that I was in no condition to stand up against that curiously vile smell. To lessen it, by getting a current of air into the cabin, I smashed in the little skylight—over which some ropes were stretched and still held the remnant of a tarpaulin, that must have been set in place while the storm was blowing which sent the ship to her account; and this so far improved matters that presently I was able to go down the companion-way, though the stench still was horridly strong.

At the bottom of the stair, the light being faint, I tripped over something; and looking down saw bones lying there with a sort of fungus partly covering them, and to the skull there still clung a mat of woolly hair plaited here and there into little braids: by which, and by the size of the bones, it seemed that a negro woman must have been left fastened

I GET INTO A SEA CHARNEL-HOUSE

into the cabin to die there after the crew had been washed overboard or had taken to the boats. But even then the business in which the ship had been engaged did not occur to me; and after hesitating for a moment I went on into the cabin, and looked about me as well as I could in the twilight for the case of bottles that I hoped to find.

The case was there, as I was pretty certain that it would be, such provision rarely being absent from old-time vessels, but all the bottles had been taken from it except an empty one—which looked as though the cabin had been opened at the last moment to fetch out supplies for the boats, and then deliberately locked fast again with the poor woman inside: an act so barbarous that it did not seem possible unless a crew of out and out devils had been in charge of the ancient craft. However, the matter which just then most concerned me was the liquor that I was in search of, that I might a little stay my stomach with it against the hunger that was tormenting me; and so I ransacked the lockers that ran across the stern of the ship and across a part of the bulkhead forward, in the faint hope that I might come upon another supply—but my search was a vain one, two of the lockers having only some mouldy clothing in them, and all the rest being filled with arms. The stock of muskets and pistols and cutlasses was so large, so far beyond any honest trader's needs, that I could not at all account for it: until the thought occurred to me that the vessel I had come aboard of had been a pirate—and that notion seemed to fit in pretty well with her crew having gone off and left the poor woman locked up in the cabin to starve. However, as I found out a little later, while my guess was a close one it still was wrong.

The four bunks, two on each side, were not enclosed, and the only door opening from the cabin was in the bulkhead forward—and worth trying because it might lead to a store-room, I thought. It was a very stout-looking door, and across it, resting in strong iron catches, were two heavy wooden bars. These puzzled me a good deal, there being no sense in barring the outside of a storeroom door in that fashion, since the door did not seem to be locked and anybody could lift the bars away. However, I got them out of their sockets without much difficulty; and after a good deal of tugging at a ring made fast in it I got the door open too — and instantly I was thrust back from the opening by an outpouring of the same vile heavy musty stench that had come up from the cabin when I staved in the hatch, only this was still ranker and more vile. And I found that the door did not lead into a little store-room, as I had fancied, but right through from the cabin to the ship's main-deck — that stretched away forward in a gloomy tunnel, as black as a cellar on a rainy

I GET INTO A SEA CHARNEL-HOUSE

night, into which I could see only for four or five yards. Indeed, but for the way that the ship chanced to be lying—with her stern toward the west, so that a good deal of light came in through the broken skylight from the ruddy sunset—I could not have seen into it at all.

But I saw far enough, and more than far enough—and the sight that I looked on sent all over me a creeping chill. Wherever the light went, skeletons were lying—with a fungus growth on the bones that gave a horrid effect of scraps of flesh still clinging to them, and the loose-lying skulls (of which a couple were close by the doorway) were covered still with a matting of woolly hair. And I could tell from the tangle that the skeletons were in—though also lying in some sort of orderly rows, because of the chains which held them fast—that the poor wretches to whom they had belonged had writhed and struggled over each other in their agony: and I could fancy what a hell that black place must have been while death was doing his work among them, they all squirming together like worms in a pot; and it seemed to me that I could hear their yells and howls—at first loud and terrible, and then growing fainter and fainter until they came to be but low groans of misery that at last ended softly in dying sighs.

The horror of it all came home to me so sharply, after I had stood there at the doorway for a moment or two held fast by a sort of ghastly fascination, that I gave a yell myself as keen and as loud as any which the poor blacks had uttered; and with that I turned about and dashed up the companion-way to the deck as hard as I could go. Nor could I bear to abide on the slave-ship, nor even near her, for the night. Very little light was left to me, but I made the most of it and went scrambling from hulk to hulk until I had put a good distance behind me—so that I not only could not see her but could not tell certainly, having twisted and turned a dozen times in my scurrying flight, in which direction she lay. And being thus rid of her, I fairly dropped—so weak and so wearied was I—on the deck of the vessel that I had come to, and lay there for a while resting, with my breath coming and going in panting sobs.

What sort of a craft I had fetched aboard of I did not dare to try to find out. Going any farther then was impossible, the twilight having slipped away almost into darkness, and whatever she might be I had to make the best of her for the night. And so I settled myself into a corner well up in her bows — that I might be as far away as possible from any grisly things that might be hid in her cabin—and did my best to go to sleep. But it was a long while, utterly weary though I was, before sleep would come to me. My stomach, being pretty well reconciled by that time to emptiness,

I GET INTO A SEA CHARNEL-HOUSE

did not bother me much; but my frightened rush away from that sickening charnel-house had left me greatly tormented by thirst, and my mind was so fevered by the horror of what I had seen that for a long while I could not stop making pictures to myself of the black wretches, chained and imprisoned, writhing under the torture of starvation and at last dying desperate in the dark. And when sleep did come to me I still had the same loathsome horrors with me in my dreams.

XXX

I COME TO THE WALL OF MY SEA-PRISON

The morning shower that waked me gave me the water that I so longed for; but it only a little refreshed me, because my chief need was food. Being past the first sharp pangs of hunger, I was in no great bodily pain; but a heavy languor was upon me that dulled me in both flesh and spirit and disposed me to give up struggling for a while, that I might enjoy what seemed to me just then to be the supreme delight of sitting still. Yet I had sense enough to know that if I surrendered to this feeling it would be the end of me; and after a little I found energy enough to throw it off.

I was helped thus to rouse myself by finding, as I looked around me with dull eyes, that the hulk I had come aboard of in such a hurry in the twilight certainly had not been wrecked for any great length of time. She was a good-sized schooner, quite modern in her build; and, although she had weathered everywhere to a pale gray, her timbers were not rotten and what was left of her cordage still was fairly sound: all of which, as I took it in slow-

THE WALL OF MY SEA-PRISON

ly, gave me hope of finding aboard of her some sort of eatable food.

But while this hope was slow to shape itself in my heavy mind, I was quick enough to act upon it when once it had taken form. With a briskness that quite astonished me I got on my feet and walked aft to the cabin—the cabin pantry being the most likely place in which to look for food put up in tins; and I was farther encouraged by finding the hatch open and the cabin itself fresh-smelling and clean. And, to my joy, the food that I hoped to find in the pantry really was there; and such a plenty of it that I could not have eaten it in a whole year.

I had the good sense to go slowly—and that was not easy, for at sight of something that would satisfy it my hunger all of a sudden woke up ragingly; but I knew that I stood a good chance of killing myself after my long fast unless I held my appetite well in hand, and so I began with a tin of peaches—opening it with a knife that I found there—and it seemed to me that those peaches were the most delicious thing that I had tasted since I was born. After they were down I went on deck again—to be out of reach of temptation—and staid there resolutely for an hour; getting at this time, and also keeping myself a little quiet, by counting six thousand slowly—and it did seem to me as though I never should get to the end! Then I had another of those delicious tins; and after a trying half hour of waiting I had a third; and then—being no longer ravenous, and no longer having the feeling of infinite emptiness—I laid down on the deck just outside the cabin scuttle and slept like a tree in winter until well along in the afternoon.

I woke as hungry as a hound, but with a comfortable and natural sort of hunger that I set myself to satisfying with good strong food: eating a tin of meat with a lively relish and without any following stomach-ache, and drinking the juice of a tin of peaches after it—there being no water fit to drink on board. My meal began to set me on my feet again; but I still felt so tired and so shaky that I decided to stay where I was until the next morning—having at last a comforting sense of security that took away my desire to hurry and made me wholly easy in my mind. And this feeling got stronger as the sun fell away westward and made a crimson bank of mist along the horizon, against which I saw the funnels of more than a dozen steamers—and so knew that the coast of my continent surely was close by. What I would do when I got to the steamers was a matter that I did not bother about. For the moment I was satisfied with the certainty that I would find aboard of them food in plenty and a comfortable place to sleep in, and that was enough. And so I did not make any plans, or even think much; but just ate

THE WALL OF MY SEA-PRISON

as much supper as I could stow away in my carcase, and then settled myself in the schooner's cabin for the night.

In the morning I was so well rested, and felt so fresh again, that I was eager to get on; and I was so light-hearted that I fell to singing as I pushed forward briskly, being full of hope once more and of airy fancies that I had only to reach the edge of the wreck-pack in order to hit upon some easy way of getting off from it out over the open sea. A little thinking would have shown me, of course, that my fancies had nothing to rest on, and that coming once more to the coast of my continent was only to be where I was when my long journey through that death-stricken mass of rottenness began; but the reaction of my spirits was natural enough after the gloom that for so long had held them, and so was the castle-building that I took to as I went onward as to what I would do with my great treasure when at last I had it safe out in the living world.

Although I did not doubt that food of some sort was to be found on board of all the vessels which I should cross that day, I guarded against losing time in looking for it by carrying along with me a couple of tins of meat—slung on my shoulders in a wrapping of canvas—and on one of these, about noon-time, I made a good meal. When I had finished it I was sorry enough that I had not brought a tin of peaches too, for the meat was pretty well salted and made me as thirsty as a fish very soon after I got it down.

But my thirst was not severe enough to trouble me greatly; and, indeed, I partly forgot it in my steadily growing excitement as I pressed forward and more and more distinctly saw the funnels of a whole fleet of steamers looming up through the golden mist ahead of me like chimneys in a sunshot London fog. And so the afternoon went by, and my crooked rough path slipped away behind me so rapidly that by a good hour before sunset I was near enough to the steamers to see not only their funnels but their hulls.

The look of one of them, and she was one of the nearest, was so familiar as I began to make her out clearly that I was sure that I had got back again to the *Hurst Castle;* for she was just about the size of the *Hurst Castle*, and was lying with her bow down in the water and her stern high in the air—and the delight of this discovery threw me into such a ferment that I quite forgot how tired I was and fairly ran across the last half dozen vessels that I had to traverse before I came under her tall side. However, when I got close to her I saw that she was not the *Hurst Castle* after all, but only another unlucky vessel that had broken her nose in collision and so had filled forward and gone sagging down by the bows.

THE WALL OF MY SEA-PRISON

As it happened, the wreck from which I had to board her was a little water-logged brig, close under her quarter, so low-lying that the tilted-up stern of the steamer fairly towered above the brig like a three-story house; and at first it seemed to me that I was about as likely to climb up a housefront as I was to climb up that high smooth wall of iron. But a part of the brig's foremast still was standing, and from it a yard jutted out to within jumping distance of the steamer's rail; and while that was not a way that I fancied—nor a way that ever I should have dared to take, I suppose, had there been any choice in the matter—up it I had to go. Hot as I was though with eagerness, I was a badly scared man as I slowly got to my feet and steadied myself for a moment on the end of the yard and then jumped for it; and a very thankful man, an instant later, when I struck the steamer's rail and fell floundering inboard on her deck—though I bruised myself in my fall pretty badly, and got an unexpected crack on the back of my head as my bag of jewels flew up and hit me with a bang.

However, no real harm was done; and I was so keen to look about me that in a moment I was on my legs again and went forward, limping a little, that I might get up on the bridge: for my strongest desire—stronger even than my longing to go in search of the water that I did not doubt I would find in the steamer's tanks—was to gaze out over the open ocean, across which I had to go in some way if ever again I was to be free.

The sun was close down on the horizon, a red ball of fire glowing through the mist, and in the mist above and over the surface of the sea below a red light shone. But as I stood on the bridge looking at this strange splendor all my hope died away slowly within me and a chill settled upon my heart. As far as ever I could see the water was covered thickly with tangled and matted weed, broken only here and there by hummocks of wreckage and by a few hulks drifting in slowly to take their places in the ranks of the dead. The almost imperceptible progress of these hulks showed how dense was the mass through which they were drifting; and showed, too, how utterly impossible it would be for me to force my way in a boat driven by oars or sails to the clear water lying far, far off. Even a steamer scarcely could have pushed through that tangle; and could not have gone twice her own length without hopelessly fouling her screw. And it seemed to me that I might better have died on one of the old rotten hulks among which I had been for so long a time wandering—where hope was not, and where I was well in the mood for dying—rather than thus to have got clear of them, and have hope come back to me, only to bring up short against the wall of my sea-prison and so find

THE WALL OF MY SEA-PRISON

myself held fast there for all the remainder of my days. And I was the more savagely bitter because I had no right whatever to be disappointed. What I saw was not new to me, and I had known what I was coming to—though I had kept down my thoughts about it—all along.

XXXI

HOW HOPE DIED OUT OF MY HEART

The steamer that I had come aboard of proved to be French; and that she had not long been abandoned I knew by finding an abundance of ice in her cold-room and a great deal of fresh meat there too. Had she been manned by a stiff-necked crew she would not have been abandoned at all. She had been in collision, and her bow-compartment was full of water; but the water had not got aft of her foremast, and except that she was down by the head a little she was not much the worse for her bang. That her captain had tried to carry on after the accident was shown by the sail that had been set in place very snugly over her smashed bows; and I greatly wondered why he had given up the fight, until I found—getting a look at her stern from one of the wrecks lying near her—that her screw was gone. This second accident evidently had been too much for her people and they had taken to the boats and left her. But I think that an English or an American crew would have stood by her, and would have succeeded in getting her towed into port—or even would have brought her in under her own sails. She was called the *Ville de Saint Remy*, and was a fine boat of about five thousand tons.

All that I had hoped to find aboard of her in the way of comforts and luxuries was there, and more too. Indeed, if a good bed, and the best of food, and excellent wines and tobacco, had been all that I wanted I very well might have settled myself on the *Ville de Saint Remy* for the balance of my days. But I almost resented the luck which had brought me all these things—for which I had been longing so keenly but a few hours before—because I did not find with them what I desired still more earnestly: the means that would enable me to get away seaward and leave them all behind. What such means would be, it is only fair to add, I could not imagine; at least, I could not imagine anything at all reasonable—for the only thing I could think of that would carry me out across that weed-covered ocean to open water was a balloon.

And so, although I fed daintily and drank of the best, and had good tobacco to cheer me after my meals, my first day aboard the *Ville de Saint Remy* was as sad a one as any that I had passed since I had come into my sea-prison; for while the daylight lasted, and I wandered about her decks looking always at the barrier of weed which held me there, I had clearly before me the impossibility of ever getting away. Only when darkness came, hiding my prison walls from me, did I become a little more cheerful—as the very human disposition to make light of difficulties when they no longer are visible began to assert itself in my mind.

Down in the comfortable cabin, well lighted and airy, I had a capital dinner—and a bottle of sound Bordeaux with it that no doubt added a good deal to my sanguine cheerfulness; and to end with I made myself some delicious coffee—over a spirit-lamp that I found in the pantry—and had with it a glass of Benedictine and a very choice cigar. And all of these luxurious refreshments of the flesh—which set me to smiling a little as I thought of the contrast that they made to my surroundings—so comforted my spirit that my gloomy thoughts left me, and I began to plan airily how I would start off in a boat well loaded with provisions and somehow or another push my way through the weed. I even got along to details: deciding that it would be quite an easy matter to open a way through the tangle over the bows of my boat with an oar—or with an axe, if need be—and then press forward by poling against the weed on each side; which seemed so feasible a method that I concluded I could accomplish readily at least a mile a day. And so, with these fine fancies dancing in my brain, I settled myself into a delightful bed; and

HOW HOPE DIED OUT OF MY HEART

as I drowsed off deliciously I had the comforting conviction that in a little while longer all my difficulties would be conquered and all my troubles at an end.

With the return of daylight, giving me an outlook over the weed-covered water again, most of my hopefulness left me along with most of my faith in my airily-made plan; but even in this colder mood it did seem to me that there was at least a chance of my pulling through — and my slim courage was strengthened by the feeling within me that unless I threw myself with all my energy into work of some sort I presently would find myself going melancholy mad. And so, but only half-heartedly, I mustered up resolution to make a trial of my poor project for getting away.

On board the *Ville de Saint Remy* there was nothing to be done. The corner-stone of my undertaking was finding a boat and launching it, and the Frenchmen — in their panic-stricken scamper from a danger that was mainly in their own lively imaginations — had carried all their boats away. It was necessary, therefore, that I should go on a cruise among the other wrecks lying around me in search of a boat still in a condition to swim; but I was very careful this time—profiting by my rough experience—to make sure before I started of my safe return. Fortunately the stern of the steamer

IN THE SARGASSO SEA

was so high out of the water that it rose conspicuously above the wrecks lying thereabouts; but to make her still more conspicuous I roused out a couple of French flags and an American flag from her signal-chest and set them at her three mastheads—giving to our own colors the place of honor on the mainmast—and so made her quite unmistakable from as far off as I could see her through the haze. And as a still farther precaution against losing myself I hunted up a hatchet to take along with me to blaze my way. All of which matters being attended to, I made a rope fast to the rail—knotting it at intervals, so that I could climb it again easily—and so slipped down the steamer's side.

My business was only with the wrecks lying along the extreme outer edge of the pack—from which alone it would be possible for me to launch a boat in the event of my finding one—but in order to get from one to the other of them I had to make so many long detours that my progress was very slow. Indeed, by the time that noon came, and I stopped to eat my dinner—which I had brought along with me, that I need not have to hunt for it—I had made less than half a mile in a straight line. And in none of the vessels that I had crossed—except on one lying so far in the pack as to be of no use to me—had I found a single boat that would swim.

HOW HOPE DIED OUT OF MY HEART

Nor had I any better luck when I went on with my search again in the afternoon. As it had been in the case of the *Hurst Castle,* so it had been, I suppose, in the case of all the wrecks which I examined that day: either their boats had been staved-in or washed overboard by tempest, or else had served to carry away their crews. But what had become of them, so far as I was concerned, made no difference—the essential matter was that they were gone. And so, toward evening, I turned backward from my fruitless journey and headed for the *Ville de Saint Remy* again—for I had found no other ship so comfortable in the course of my explorations—and got safe aboard of her just as the sun was going down.

That night I had not much comfort in the good dinner that I set out for myself—though I was glad enough to get it, being both hungry and tired—and I only half plucked up my spirits over my coffee and cigar. But still, as the needs of my body were gratified, my mind got so far soothed and refreshed that I held to my purpose—which had been pretty much given over when I came back tired and hungry after my vain search—and I went to bed resolute to begin again my explorations on the following day.

But when the morning came and I set off—though I had a good breakfast inside of me, and such a store of food by me as fairly would have set me dancing with delight only a week before—I was in low spirits and went at my work rather because I was resolved to push through with it than because I had any strong hope that it would give me what I desired.

This time—having already examined the wrecks for near a mile northward along the edge of the pack—I set my course for the south; and again, until late in the afternoon, I worked my way from ship to ship—with long detours inland from time to time in order to get around some break in the coast-line—and on all of them the result was the same: not a boat did I find anywhere that was not so riven and shattered as to be beyond all hope of repair. And at nightfall I came back once more to the *Ville de Saint Remy* wearied out in body and utterly dispirited in mind.

Even after I had eaten my dinner and was smoking at my ease in the cheerfully lighted cabin, sitting restfully in a big arm-chair and with every sort of material comfort at hand, I could not whip myself up to hoping again. It was true that I had not exhausted the possibilities of finding the boat that I desired so eagerly, for my search along the coast-line had extended for only about a mile each way; but in my down-hearted state it seemed to me that my search had gone far enough to settle definitely that what I wanted was not to be found. And this brought down on me heavily the convic-

HOW HOPE DIED OUT OF MY HEART

tion that my prison—though it was the biggest, I suppose, that ever a man was shut up in—must hold me fast always: and with that feeling in it there no longer was room for hope also in my heart.

XXXII

I FALL IN WITH A FELLOW-PRISONER

WHEN I had finished my breakfast the next morning I faced the worst thing which I had been forced to face since I had been cast prisoner into the Sargasso Sea: a whole day of idleness without hope. Until then there had not been an hour—save when I was asleep—that I had not been doing something which in some way I had hoped would better my condition temporarily, or would tend toward my deliverance. But that morning I was without such spurs to effort and there was absolutely nothing for me to do. My condition could not be improved by making my home on another vessel; it was doubtful, indeed, if in all the wreck-pack I could find a home so comfortable and so abundantly stocked with the best provisions as I had found aboard of the *Ville de Saint Remy*. As for working farther for my deliverance, I had set that behind me after my experience during the two preceding days. And so I brought a steamer-chair out on the deck and sat in it smoking, idle and hopeless, gazing straight out before me with a

I FALL IN WITH A FELLOW-PRISONER

dull steadfastness over the very gently undulating surface of the weed-covered sea.

After a while, tiring of sitting still, I began to pace the deck slowly; and I was so heavy with my sorrow that I could not think clearly, but had only in my mind a confused feeling that I was taking the first of a series of walks such as wild animals imprisoned take endlessly back and forth behind the bars that shut them in. And from this I went on to thinking, still in the same confused way, that the wild animals at least were not outcast in their captivity—having living people and living beasts around them, and the pleasure of hearing living sounds—while one of the worst things about my prison was the absolute dead silence that hung over it like a dismal cloud. And perhaps it was because my thoughts happened at that moment to be set to take notice of such matters that I fancied I heard a very faint sound of scratching and an instant later a still fainter little cry.

I was standing just then close to the water-line on the deck forward, beside a covered hatch that seemed to lead to what had been the quarters of the crew; and it was from beneath this hatch, I was certain, that the sounds came. Slight though the noise was, it greatly startled me; and at the same time it aroused in me the strangely-thrilling hope that there possibly might be a living man still aboard of the steamer and that I would be no longer horribly alone. Yet I would not suffer myself too much to give room to this happy hope, for the little faint scratching—which I heard again presently—was not the sort of noise that a man shut in would be likely to make; nor did the little plaintive sound seem like a human cry. But the matter was one to be investigated in a hurry, and with an energy quite astonishing, in comparison with my lassitude of a moment before, I got the hatch open and leaned down it, listening; and then I heard the scratching so plainly that I hurried down the stair.

The between-decks was well enough lighted by a good-sized skylight, and the place that I had got into had fixed tables set in it and seemed to be the mess-room of the crew. Doors opened out from it both fore and aft; and from behind the after door —so plainly that I had no difficulty in placing it— came the scratching sound that I was pursuing: and with it came the cries again, and this time so distinctly as to shatter my hope of finding a human being there, but at the same time to make me, for all my sorrow, almost smile. For the cry was a very long and plaintive m-i-i-a-a-u! And the next moment, when I had the door open, a great black cat came out upon me—so overcome with delight at meeting a human being again that he was almost choking with his gurgling purr. Indeed the extravagant joy of the poor lonely creature was as

I FALL IN WITH A FELLOW-PRISONER

great as mine would have been had I found a man there—and he manifested it by lunging sidewise against my legs, and by standing up on his hind paws and reaching his fore paws up to my knees and clutching them, and then with a spring he climbed right up me—all the while choking with his great gurgling purring—and was not satisfied until he found himself bundled close against my breast as I held him tight in my arms. And on my side—after I had gulped down my first disappointment because it was only a cat who was my fellow-prisoner—I was as glad to meet him as he was to meet me; and I am not ashamed to say that I fairly cried over him—as a warm rush of joy went over me at finding myself at last, after being for so long a time surrounded only by the dead, in the company of a living creature; and a creature which showed toward me by every means that a brute beast could compass its gratitude and its love.

And I must add without delay that my cat's affection for me was wholly disinterested; at least, I am sure that he loved me—from the first moment of our encounter—not because he wanted me to do something for him, but because he longed, as I did, for human companionship and was filled up with happiness because he had found again a human friend. As I discovered upon investigation, his prison had been the galley in which food for the crew had been cooked; and upon the odds and ends left there he had fared very well indeed—not overeating himself by gobbling down all his food in a hurry, and then dying of starvation, as a dog would have done, but temperately eating for his daily rations only what his sustenance required; and for drink he had had a pot partly full of what had been hot water that stood upon the galley stove. But I also must add that this coarse fare was not at all to his liking; and that thereafter he ordered me around pretty sharply, in his own way, and insisted always upon my providing him with dainty food.

It was a good thing for the cat, certainly, that I had found him; for his stock of provisions was pretty nearly exhausted, and in a little while longer he would have come to a dismal end. But my finding him was a still better thing for me. When I first heard his faint little scratching, and his still fainter plaintive little call for help, I was so deep in my despairing melancholy that my reason was in a fair way to go, and with it all farther effort on my part to set myself free. From that desperate state my small adventure with him roused me, which was a good deal to thank him for; but I had more to thank him for still.

In the little time that I had been aboard of the *Ville de Saint Remy*—my days having been passed away from her—I had made no exploration of her

I FALL IN WITH A FELLOW-PRISONER

interior beyond her cabin and the region in which were carried her cabin stores; which latter were so abundant as to set me at my ease for an indefinite period in regard to food. But this meeting with my fellow-prisoner so stirred me up, and put such fresh spirit into me, that I began to think of having a general look all over her: that I might in a way take stock of my belongings and at the same time have something to occupy my mind—for I knew that to sit down idly again would be only again to fall back into despair. And so, my cat going with me—and, indeed, making a good deal of a convenience of me, for he by no means would walk on his own legs but insisted upon jumping up on my shoulder and going that way as a passenger—I set off on my round.

As well as I could make out from what I found on board of her—for her papers either had been carried away or were stowed in some place which I did not discover—the *Ville de Saint Remy* had been bound outward to some colonial port and carried a cargo of general stores. When I got her hatches off—though that came later—I saw in one place a lot of wheelbarrows, and some heavy wagons stowed with their wheels inside of them, and some machinery for threshing along with a portable steam-engine; and in another place were boxes which seemed to have dry-goods in them, and a great many cases of wines, and some very big cases that evidently contained pianos—and so on with a great lot of stuff such as the people of a flourishing colony would be likely to need.

But in my round that morning with the cat on my shoulders—for he was not content to remain perched on one of them quietly, but kept passing from one to the other with affectionate rubs against the back of my head, and all the while purring as hard as he could purr—I did not get below the main-deck except into the engine-room, my attention being given to finding out fully what the steamer had on board of her in the way of work-shops and tools: for already, with my renewed cheerfulness, the notion was beginning to take hold of me that I might set to work and build a boat for myself—and so make what I could not find. And, indeed, I don't doubt that I should have set myself to this big undertaking—for the appointments of the vessel were admirably complete and everything that I wanted for my work was there—had not a bigger, but a more promising, undertaking presented itself to me and so turned my efforts into another way.

XXXIII

I MAKE A GLAD DISCOVERY

It was directly to my cat that I owed the great piece of good fortune that then came to me: but I must confess that he was an unwilling agent in the matter, and probably wished himself well out of it, the immediate result in his case being rather a bad squeeze to one of his fore paws.

We had been examining the machine-shop, the cat and I, and whatever his views about it may have been mine were of great satisfaction; for when I had got the dead-lights unscrewed so that I could see well about me I had been delighted by finding there everything that my boat-building project required. Indeed, I almost fancied myself back again in one of the work-shops of the Stevens Institute, so well was the place fitted and supplied —a completeness probably due to the fact that the *Ville de Saint Remy* was intended for long voyages to out-of-the-way ports, and very well might have to depend upon her own resources for important repairs.

It was as we were leaving the machine-shop to

continue our round of investigations that my cat suddenly took it into his head to jump down from my shoulders and stretch his own legs a little; and away he scampered—being much given to such frisking dashes, as I later discovered, though for the next week or so after that one he went limping on three legs mighty soberly—first down the deck aft, and then past me and up a dark passage leading toward the bows; and I, being pretty well accustomed to cat habits, stood waiting until he should have his fun out and so come back again with a miau by way of "if you please" to be taken up into my arms. But he did not come back in any great hurry, and off in the darkness I could hear his paws padding about briskly; and then there was silence for a moment; and then he broke out into a loud miauling which showed that he was in trouble of some sort and also in pain.

As there was no helping him until I could see what was the matter with him, I hurried first into the machine-shop for a wrench, and then went forward into that dark place cautiously—until by a glint of light on the ship's side I made out where a port was, and so got loose the deadlight and could look around. What I saw was my poor cat in such a pickle that I did not in the least blame him for crying out about it; he having, as it seemed, made an unlucky jump upon some small bars of iron which were lying loose and disorderly, with the

I MAKE A GLAD DISCOVERY

one on which he landed balanced so nicely that it had turned suddenly and jammed fast his paw. And so he was anchored there very painfully, and was telling what he thought about it in the most piercing yowls.

Fortunately it was an easy matter to let him loose from the trap that he had got into; but even while I was doing it—and before I picked him up to look at his hurt and to comfort him—I gave a shout of delight on my own account that was a good deal louder than any of my poor cat's yells of pain. For there before me was a very stout-looking and large steam-launch—thirty-two feet over all, as I found when I came to measure her—stowed snugly in a cradle set athwart-ship and looking all ready to be put overboard into the sea. And at finding in this unexpected fashion what I had been so long looking for, and had quite done with hoping for, it is no wonder that I shouted with joy.

My cat coming limping to me to be pitied and cared for, holding up his pinched paw and with little miaus asking for my sympathy quite like a Christian, I had first of all to give him my attention. But his hurt was not a very serious one—the flesh not being cut, and no bones broken—and when I had comforted him as well as I could, until I got him soothed a little, I put him down out of my arms that I might examine carefully my great prize; but first of all opening all the ports so that I might have plenty of light for what I wanted to do.

Coming to this deliberate survey, I found that the launch truly enough was complete, but that she was very far from being ready to take the water; for while all her parts were there—and even duplicates of her more important pieces, in readiness against a break-down—most of her fittings and all of her machinery was lying inside of her boxed for transportation; being arranged that way, I suppose, because she would have been far too heavy to swing into the snug place where I found her and out again with everything bolted fast. She was a very beautiful little boat, evidently intended for a pleasure craft—but very strong and seaworthy, too; and it no doubt was to keep her in good order for delivery that she had been stowed betweendecks for the long voyage. Indeed, only with a steam-winch and a good many men to handle her, could she have been got down there; and the first of my uncomfortable thoughts about her, of the many that I had first and last, came while I was taking stock of her equipment—as I fell to wondering how in the world I should manage, with only a cat to help me, ever to get her overboard into the sea.

As to assembling her parts, and so making her ready for cruising, I had no doubts whatever.

I MAKE A GLAD DISCOVERY

That piece of work was directly in the line of my training and I felt entirely secure about it; but even on that score I quaked a good deal at the size of the contract to be taken by a single pair of hands, and at thought of the long, long while that would be required to carry it through. Yet the hope that came with finding this boat put such heart into me that my spirits did not go down far. Working on her—aside from the pleasure that any man with a natural love for mechanics finds in serious and difficult labor with his hands—would be a constant delight to me because of what it would be leading to; and in every moment of my work I would have to sustain me the thought that each rivet set in place and each bolt fastened brought me appreciably nearer to being set free.

Having cursorily finished with the boat, I continued my survey to her surroundings; that I might plan roughly my scheme of work upon her, and that I might plan also for getting her launched when my work upon her should be done. She was stowed on the main-deck—in a place that probably was intended for the use of third-class passengers, when such were carried—and the machine-shop was so close to her that in the matter of fetching tools and so on my steps would be well saved. Directly over her was the forward hatch; through which she had been lowered and set in place in the cradle previously made ready for her, and there fixed firm and fast. For a moment I had the fancy that I might get up steam to work the donkey-engine and so hoist her out again by that same way, and overboard too. But a very little reflection showed me that this airily formed plan must be abandoned, as all my work on her then would have to be done far away from the machine-shop and with the additional disadvantage that through the long time that certainly must pass before I could get her finished she would lie open to the daily heavy rains. And then I had the much more reasonable notion — though the amount of extra labor that it involved was not encouraging to contemplate—that I would do my work on her where she lay; and when I had finished her that I would cut loose a sufficient number of plates from the side of the steamer to make a hole big enough to get her overboard that way.

But having the hatch directly over where she was lying, though I could not get her up through it, made my undertaking a good deal easier and more comfortable for me. Even with all the ports open I would have had but little light to work by; and, what was of even more importance in that hot misty region, I would have had little fresh air—and still less when I had set a-going my forge. But with the hatch off I could have all the light that I needed and as much fresh air as was to be had—with the advantage that the hatch could be set in

I MAKE A GLAD DISCOVERY

place every night when I went off duty and not opened again in the morning until the rain was at an end: so preserving my machinery against the rust that pretty much would have ruined it—for all that it was well tallowed—had my slow building gone on in the open air.

My preliminary investigations being thus well ended, and the morning ended too, I piped all hands to dinner; that is to say, I whistled to my cat—who had been sitting still and watching me pretty solemnly, his friskiness being for the time taken out of him by the pain in his paw—and when he perceived that I was paying some attention to him again he came limping to me on his three good legs and said with a miau that if I pleased he would prefer going to his dinner in my arms. And when I picked him up—as, indeed, I had to, for he positively insisted upon my carrying him—he forgot about his hurt and fell to purring to me at a great rate and to making little gentle thrusts against my arm with the fore paw that was sound. And so we went aft in great friendship and contentment and had a gay dinner together: the cat sitting on the table opposite to me with all possible decorum—but manifesting his daintiness by refusing to eat anything but tinned chicken, and only the white meat at that!

XXXIV

I END A GOOD JOB WELL, AND GET A SET-BACK

When my meal was finished I set myself first of all to getting off the hatch beneath which my boat lay; and this proved to be a bigger job than I had counted upon—each of its sections being so heavy that I could not manage it without tackle, and even with tackle the work took me a good hour. My plan of operations had included removing the hatch every morning and setting it back again every night, but when I found how much energy and time would be wasted in that way I changed my front a little and got at the same result along another line. All that I needed was a covering for the hatch that would keep the rain out; and what I did, therefore, was to knock together a light grating of wood to fit over it—sloping the grating downward on each side from a sort of a ridge pole—on which a tarpaulin could be stretched; and in that way I got shortly to a water-tight covering for my hatch that I could shift back and forth quickly and without any trouble at all. But the whole of what remained of the afternoon was spent

A GOOD JOB, AND A SET-BACK

in getting that piece of preliminary work finished to my mind.

The next morning I set myself to the examination of the stuff stowed in the boat—the several parts which I would have to put together in order to make my craft ready for the sea—and for this job also a great deal of preliminary arrangement was required. Many of the pieces—as the boiler, the cylinder, the shaft, the screw, and the sections of the cabin—were too heavy for me to lift without tackle; and as they all had to be got out and arranged in order ready for use, and then in due course put aboard the boat one at a time in their proper places, I first of all had to set up some sort of lifting apparatus to take the place of a crane.

In this matter the open hatch directly over the boat again was a help to me. Across it, running fore and aft, I stretched a heavy wire rope on which I had placed a big block for a traveller, and carrying the end of the rope forward to the capstan I fell to work with the hand-bars and got it strained so taut that it was like a bar of iron. Then to the traveller block I made fast my hoisting tackle—and so was able to swing up the heavy pieces from where they were stowed, and to run them along the taut rope until they were clear of the boat on either side, and then to let them down upon the deck: where they would remain until a reversal of this process would lift them up again and set them in place as they were required. But even with my tackle—and double tackle in the case of the heavier pieces—this was a back-breaking job that took up the whole of three days.

However, I finished it at last, and had the boat clear and all the pieces so arranged that as I needed them they would be ready to my hand; and the examination that I was able to make of them, and of the boat too after I had her empty, gave very satisfactory results. All the parts were there, and all numbered so carefully that they could have been assembled by much less skilful hands than mine; while the hull of the boat was completely finished, and the sockets and rivet-holes for attaching her fittings were all as they should be in her frame. Farther, I could see by the little scratches here and there on her iron-work that she had been set up and then taken apart again; and so was sure that all was smooth for her coming together in the right way. But, for all that I had such plain sailing before me in the actual work of refitting her, my courage went down a little as I perceived what a big contract I had taken, and what a very long time must pass before I could pull it through.

Moreover, I saw that while the boat was well built for pleasure cruising in smooth water—and, indeed, was so stout in her frame that she would stand a great deal of knocking about without being the worse for it—she by no means was prepared for the chances of an ocean voyage. Except where her little cabin and engine-room would be—the two filling about half of her length amidships—she was entirely open; and while the frame of her cabin was stoutly built, that part of it intended to rise above the rail was arranged for sliding glass windows—which would be smashed in a moment by a heavy dash of sea. It was clear, therefore, that in addition to setting her up on the lines planned for her—a big job and a long job to start with—there was a lot more for me to do. To fit her for my purposes it would be necessary to cover her cabin windows with planking; to deck her over forward in order to have my stores under cover as well as to guard against shipping enough water to swamp her in rough weather; and finally to rig her with a mast and sail upon which to fall back for motive-power in the event of my running out of coal. This additional work would not, in one way, present any difficulties—it being in itself simple and easy of accomplishment; but in another way it was not pleasant to contemplate, since the doing of it all single-handed would increase very greatly the time which must pass before I could start upon my voyage. However, as consideration of that phase of the matter only tended to discourage me, I put it out of sight as well as I was able and set myself with a will to finishing my preliminary work—of which there still was a good deal to do.

The steamer's machine-shop, as I have said, was unusually well fitted and supplied; but even in the short time that the vessel had been lying abandoned in that reeking atmosphere rust had so coated everything not shut up in lockers that all the tools in the racks and the fittings of the lathe —although the lathe had an oil-cloth hood over it —had to be cleaned before they could be used: a job that kept me busy with the grind-stone, and emery-cloth, and oiled cotton-waste, for a good long while. And after that I had to get the forge in order, and to bring up fuel for it from the coal bunkers. And in attending to all these various matters the time slipped away so quickly that a whole week had passed before I had done.

But I must say that as the cat and I labored together—though his labors were confined to cheering me by following me about on three legs wherever I went, and pretty much all the while talking to me in his way so that I should not fail to take notice of him—I got more and more light-hearted; which was natural enough, seeing that what I was doing in itself interested me and so made the time pass quickly, and that I had also a great swelling under-current of hope as I thought of what my slow-going work would bring me to in the end.

When at last I fairly got started at my building

A GOOD JOB, AND A SET-BACK

I was in a still more cheerful mood—there being such a sense of definite accomplishment as I set each piece in its place, and such a comfort in the tangible advance that I was making, that half the time I was singing as I made my bolts and rivets fast. But for all my cheerfulness I had a plenty of trouble over what I was doing; and I was sorry enough that I had not somebody beside my cat to help me, or that I myself had not another pair or two of hands.

Almost at the start, when I began to swing the pieces of machinery inboard, I found that I had still another bit of preliminary work to attend to before I could go on. My travelling tackle crossing the boat amidships had worked well enough in getting the stuff out of her, but when I came to hoisting the parts aboard and setting them exactly in their places, and holding them steady while I made fast the rivets, it would not in any way serve my turn. What I had to do was to stretch another wire rope across the hatch—at right angles with and a couple of feet above the first one, and parallel with the boat's keel—and to rig on this two travellers, to one or the other of which I could transfer each piece as I got it inboard and so run it along until I had it exactly over the place where it was to be made fast. But I was a whole day in attending to this matter—and it was only one of the many makeshifts to which I had to resort to accomplish what was too much for my unaided strength; and in meeting such like side difficulties I lost in all a good many days.

But though my work went very slowly, and now and then was stopped short for a while by some obstacle that had to be overcome in any rough and ready way that I could think of, I did get on; and at last I had my boat together on the lines that her builders had planned. Yet while, in a way, she was finished, there still was a weary lot to do to her to fit her for my purposes; and in decking her over, and in making her cabin solid, and in fitting a mast and sail to her, I spent almost two months more.

All this work went slowly because I had to spend nearly as much time in making ready for what I wanted to do as in doing it. Before I began my planking I had to rip up from the steamer's deck the material for it; and this was a hard job in itself and did not give me what I wanted when it was done—for while the stuff served well enough for my beams and braces it was clumsily heavy for the decking of my little launch. But it had to answer, and in the end I got it well in place and the joints so tightly caulked that I was sure of having a dry hold. And that my deck might the more easily turn the water in a sea way I made it flush with the rail; and I had no hatch in it—arranging to get to the hold by a scuttle that I set in the forward end of the cabin—and that gave me a still better chance of keeping dry below.

For my mast I got down one of the top-gallant masts—and I had a close shave to coming down with it and so ending my adventures right there. The best way that I could think of to manage this piece of work—and I have not since thought of any way better—was to make fast a line to the lower end of the top-gallant mast just above the cap of the topmast and to carry this line through the top-block and so down to the deck, and there to pass it through another block to the capstan and haul it taut and stop it; and when all that was in order, and the stays cut, to get up into the cross-trees and saw through the spar just below where I had whipped it with my line. My expectation was that as the spar parted and fell it would be held hanging by my tackle until I could get down to the deck again and lower it away; and that really was what did happen—only as it fell there was a bit of slack line to take up, and this gave such a tremendous jerk to the cross-trees that I was within an ace of being shaken out of them and of going down to the deck with a bang. But I didn't—which is the main thing—and I did get my mast. It was a good deal heavier than my boat could stand, and I had to spend a couple of days in taking it down with a broad-axe and in finishing it with a plane until I got it as it should be; and from the flag-staff at the steamer's stern I got out with very little trouble a good boom and gaff.

After that I had only my sail to fit; and as I did not trouble myself to make a very neat job of it this did not take me long. Indeed, I grudged the time that I spent on my mast and sail—close upon a fortnight, altogether—more than any like amount of time that I gave to my task; for my hope was strong that I would not need a sail at all, but would be able to manage—by a way that I had thought of—to carry enough coal with me to make my voyage under steam. But I was not leaving anything to chance — so far as chances could be foreseen — in the adventure that I was about to make, and so I got my sail-power all ready to fall back upon in case my steam-power failed. And when that bit of work was finished I was full of a joyful light-heartedness; for my boat in every way was ready for the water, and I was come at last to the good ending of my long job.

That night I made a feast in celebration of what I had accomplished, and in hope of my greater good fortune that I believed was soon to come—with a place duly set on the opposite side of the table for my only guest, and with a champagne-glass beside his plate to hold his unsweetened condensed milk (for which, when I found it among the ship's stores, he manifested a strong partiality) that he might lap properly his responses to the

A GOOD JOB, AND A SET-BACK

toasts which I pledged him in champagne. And I don't suppose that a man and a cat ever had a merrier meal anywhere than we had in that queer place for it that evening; nor that any two friends ever were happier together than we were when, our feast being ended, he went through his various tricks—of which he had learned a great many, and with a wonderful quickness, after his paw got well—and then settled himself for a snooze on my lap while I sat smoking my cigar and thinking that at last I had saws through my prison bars.

And it was while I was sitting in that state of placid happiness that suddenly I was brought up all standing by the reflection—and why it had not come sooner to me is a mystery—that a dozen turns of the screw of my launch in that weed-covered ocean would be enough to foul it hopelessly, and so at the very start to cut short the voyage under steam that I had planned.

XXXV

I AM READY FOR A FRESH HAZARD OF FORTUNE

For a while after this black thought came to me I was pretty much beaten by it; but when I got steadier—and had finished kicking myself for a fool because I had not foreseen it all along—I perceived that the odds were not wholly against me, after all. I had, at least, a sea-worthy boat in which to make my venture, and therefore was as well off as I had hoped to be when I had set about looking for one; and if the plan that I had formed worked out in practice—if I could manage to force a passage through the tangle by alternately working over the bow of my boat to break up the weed, and over the sides to pole my boat forward—I was a great deal better off than I had hoped to be: for should I win my way to open water I would have steam as well as sail power at my command.

But while this more reasonable view of the situation comforted me, it did not satisfy me. The difficulty of working myself along in that slow fashion I foresaw would be so enormous that I very well might die of sheer exhaustion before I got clear of

A FRESH HAZARD OF FORTUNE

the weed-tangle—which must extend outward, as I knew from my guess at the time that I had taken in drifting in through it, for a very long way. What I had been counting upon ever since I had found the launch was in having part of the work, and the heaviest part, done by her engine; my part to be the breaking of a passage, while the motive power was to be supplied by the screw. But of course if the screw fouled, as it certainly would foul with the loose weed all around it, that would be the end of my hopeful plan.

This consideration of the matter reduced it to a definite problem. What was needed was some sort of protection for the screw that would keep the weed away from it and yet would allow it to work freely: and, having the case thus clearly stated, the thought presently occurred to me that I could secure this protection by building out from the stern of the boat, so that the screw would be enclosed in it, some sort of an iron cage. That arrangement, I conceived, would meet the requirements of the case fully; and being come to my conclusion I resigned myself to still another long delay while I carried my plan into execution, and so went to bed at last hopefully—but well knowing that this fresh piece of work that I had cut out for myself would be hard to do.

I certainly did not overestimate the amount of labor involved in my cage-building. I was a good three weeks over it. But I was kept up to the collar by my conviction that without the cage I had no chance of succeeding in my project; and so I got it finished at last. And then I considered that my boat really was ready to take the water; and the cat and I had another banquet in celebration of the long step that we had taken toward our deliverance—only this time I did not give an altogether free rein to my rejoicing, being fearful that some other difficulty might present itself suddenly and bring me up again with a round turn.

The boat being ready—for I could think of nothing more to do to her—I had still to launch her, and the first step toward that end was breaking out a section in the steamer's side. Luckily the stock of cold-chisels aboard the *Ville de Saint Remy* was a good one; but I dulled them all twice over—and weary work at the grindstone I had sharpening them again—before I had chipped away the bindings of those endless rivets and had the satisfaction of seeing the big section of iron plate between two of her iron ribs pitch outboard and splash down through the weed into the sea.

As I have said, the bow compartment of the steamer was full of water, and this brought her main-deck so low down forward that the boat had only to be slid out almost on a level through the hole that I had made. But to slide her that way —which seems easy, because I have happened to put it glibly—was quite a different thing. With steam power to work the capstan I could have got the boat overboard in no time; but without steam power the launching went desperately slowly, and was altogether the hardest piece of work that I had to do in the whole of my long hard job.

The boat had stood all along in the cradle that had been built to hold her steady for the voyage. This was a very stout wooden framework built up from two heavy beams joined by cross-pieces, and all so well bolted together that it was very solid and firm. In this the boat rested snugly and was held fast by rope lashings; and the cradle itself—resting on the lower hatch and projecting on each side of it—was lashed to the hatch ringbolts so as to be safe against shifting in a heavy sea. I could have removed the cradle by taking it to pieces, but that would not have helped matters; and the plan that I decided upon—liking it better because all this wood-work around and under the boat would protect her from harm as she went overboard—was to weight the cradle with iron bars that would cause it to sink away from beneath the boat when they took the water, and then to work it up with jack-screws until I could get rollers under it and so send them both together over the side.

How long I worked over this job I really do not know; but I do know that at the time it seemed as though it never would come to an end. First of all I had the rollers to make from another topgallant mast that I got down, and when these were finished I had to go at the frame of the cradle with a pair of jack-screws and raise it, by fractions of an inch, until I could get my rollers under it one at a time. I think that it was the deadly dullness of this jack-screw work that I most resented—the stupid monotony of doing precisely the same sort of utterly wearying work all day long and for day after day. But in the end I got it finished: all my rollers properly in place, and the cradle made fast to hold it from starting before I was ready to have it go—although of that there was not much danger, for while the steamer had a decided pitch forward she lay on an even keel.

At first I was for sending my boat overboard the minute that I got the last roller under her; but I had the sense, luckily, to take a reef in this brisk intention as the thought struck me that I must have open water to launch her in or else very likely have boat and cradle together stuck fast in the weed. And so I set myself to clearing a little pool into which I could launch her; and as I carried this work on I came quickly to a realizing sense of what was before me when I should begin to break a way through the weed for my boat's passage, and to the conviction that had I tried to make my voyage without steam to help me I never should have got through at all.

A FRESH HAZARD OF FORTUNE

In point of fact, the weed was so thick and so firmly matted together that I almost could walk on it; and when I had knocked loose a couple of doors from their hinges and had thrown them overboard—taking two, so that I might move one ahead of the other as my cutting advanced—I had firm enough standing place from which I could slash away. So tough was the mass that I was a whole day in uncovering a space less than forty feet long by twenty broad; and when my launching-pool was finished it had the look of a little pond in a meadow surrounded by solid banks.

All this showed me that even with the screw to push while I cleared a way for the boat's passage I should have my hands full; but it also put into my head a notion that helped me a good deal in the end. This was to rig on the straight stem of my boat a set of guide-bars projecting forward in which I could work perpendicularly a cross-cut saw, and in that way to cut a slit in the weed—which would be widened by the boat's nose thrusting into it as the screw shoved her onward, and so would enable me to squeeze along. And as this was a matter easy of accomplishment—being only to double over a couple of iron bars so that there would be a slit a half inch wide for the saw to travel in, and to bolt them fast to the top and bottom of the boat's stem—I did it immediately; and it worked so well when I came to try it that I was glad enough that I had had so lucky a thought. Indeed, had I known how well it would turn out I should have gone a step farther and rigged my saw to run by steam power—setting up a frame in the bows to hold a wheel carrying a pin on which the saw could play and to which I could make fast a bar from my piston-rod—and in that way saved myself from the longest bit of back-breaking work that ever I had to do. But that was a piece of foresight that came afterward, and so did me no good.

When my guide-bars were in place, and the saw made ready to slip into them by taking off one of its handles—and I had still a spare saw to fall back upon in the event of the first one breaking—my boat was ready to go overboard into the open water, where she would lie while I put aboard of her my coal and stores. But the work that was before me, as I thus came close to it, loomed up very large; and so did the doubts which beset me as to how my voyage would end. Indeed, it was in a spirit far from exultant that at last I cut the lashings which held the cradle; and then with the tackle that I had ready got the heavy mass started—and in a couple of minutes had my boat safely overboard and floating free, as the cradle sunk away from under her, carried down by its lading of iron bars.

But, whatever was to come of it, the launching of

A FRESH HAZARD OF FORTUNE

my boat started me definitely along a fresh line of adventure, and whether I liked it or not I had to make the best of it: and so I stated the case to my cat—who had got scared and run off into a corner while the launching was in progress — when he came marching up to me and seated himself beside me gravely, as I stood in the break in the steamer's side looking down at the boat that I hoped would set us free.

XXXVI

HOW MY CAT PROMISED ME GOOD LUCK

WHAT would have been most useful to me as foresight, but was only aggravating to me as hindsight—which happened to be the way that I got it—was the very sensible notion that I might have put all of my stores, and even a good part of my coal, aboard the boat before she was decked over and launched. A few tons more or less would have made no difference in moving her; but having to put those extra tons aboard of her over the side of the steamer, and then to drag them through the cabin and through the awkward little hatch, and at last to stow them by the light of a lantern in her stiflingly close hot hold—all that made a lot of difference to me. However, I could not foresee everything; and I think, on the whole, that I really did foresee most of what I wanted pretty well.

Of provisions I took along enough to last me, by a rough calculation, for three months; being pretty well satisfied that unless within that time I got through the weed-tangle to open water—over which

I could make my way to land, or on which I might fall in with a passing vessel—I never would get free at all. And I was the more disposed to keep down my lading of provisions because I wanted every scrap of room that I could save for my cargo of coal. But my stores were plentiful for the term that I had fixed upon, and the best and the most nourishing—save that I could not take fresh meat with me—that the *Ville de Saint Remy* had on board; and I did not forget to take a good supply of the tinned chicken and the condensed milk of which my dainty cat was so fond. As for water—beside having my condenser to fall back upon—I felt pretty sure that until I got well out toward the open sea I could trust to the morning rains. But for all that I carried two barrels with me—filled fresh the last thing before I started—stowed in the well of the boat aft of the cabin; and there too I carried a couple of ten-gallon tins of oil for my lanterns and lamps.

My bone-breaking job was getting my coal aboard. For ease in handling and in stowing it—though I lost a little room that way—I put it in canvas sacks, of which I luckily found some bales in the steamer's cargo. These I swung up from the engine-room by the cinder-tackle to the main deck; and having got them that far I packed them on my back to the break in the steamer's side where my boat was lying and tumbled them aboard of her, and then dragged them along to where I stowed them in her hold. On my coal holding out at least until I got through the weed—for on open water I could lay a course under sail—the success of my adventure wholly depended; and knowing that, I filled my boat with all that I dared to put into her—loading the last twenty bags on her deck and on the roof of her cabin, to be used before I drew on my main supply.

But while this lading was a big one it did not satisfy me; and the only way that I could think of to better it was to build a long and narrow raft that I could stow as much more on and tow after me in the boat's wake. This was a big undertaking, but I had to face it and to carry it through: lowering down three spars (in managing which I used a treble-purchase to swing them clear, and eased them down with a couple of turns of the rope still around the capstan), and when I had them over the side in a pool that I had cleared for them I lashed them strongly together and decked them over with some of the state-room doors. This gave me a raft sixty feet long, or thereabouts, but narrower than my boat; and to make it follow the boat still more easily I set a V-shaped cut-water at its bows to turn the weed. To be sure, it was a clumsy thing, but it well enough served my turn.

On this structure I was able to carry a prodigious quantity of coal—more than I had on the

MY CAT PROMISED ME GOOD LUCK

boat, by a good deal; but by a little planning in advance I arranged matters so that the lading of it was not so hard a piece of work—though in all conscience it was hard enough—as the lading of my boat had been. What I did was to clear a pool in the weed for it and to build it directly beneath the outhang of the cinder-tackle; and having that apparatus ready to my hand I swung my bags of coal up from the engine-room, and then out along the traveller, and then lowered them away—and so had only to stow them on the raft when they were down. But there was only one of me to do all this—to fill each bag in the bunkers and to bring it to the engine-room, to make it fast there to the tackle, to come on deck and haul it up and set it overboard, to go down the side and set it in place, and then back to the bunkers again for the next round—and so I spent a week in doing what three men could have done in a day. And I was a tired man and a grimy man when I got this piece of work finished; but I was comforted by knowing that I had as much coal in my sea-stock as I possibly could have use for—and so I scrubbed myself clean in the steamer's bath-room and was easy in my mind. But it was a good long while before I got the aches out of my bones.

During my last week aboard the *Ville de Saint Remy* I had steam up in my boat and my engine at work during the greater part of each day: as was necessary, the engine being new, in order to get the machinery to running smoothly, and to set right anything that might be wrong while I still had the steamer's machine-shop to turn to for repairs. However, the engine proved to be a well-made one, and except that I had to tighten a joint here and there and to repack the piston I had nothing to rectify; and what still more pleased me was to find that my cage answered to keep the screw from fouling, and that my plan for sawing a way through the weed—which I tested by running a little distance from the steamer through the thick of it—worked well too. But because of the great friction to be overcome as the boat opened a way for itself in the dense soft mass my progress was desperately slow; and I had to comfort me the reflection that it would be still slower when I got regularly under way and had in addition to the dead thrust forward of the boat the dead drag after it of the raft.

Slow or fast, though, I had no choice in the matter. With the means at my command, I had done all that I could do to enable me to climb the walls of my prison—if I may put it that way—and there remained only to muster what pluck I had to help me and to abide by the result. This was the view of the situation that I presented to my cat—for I had got into the habit of talking to him quite as much as he talked to me—while we sat at sup-

MY CAT PROMISED ME GOOD LUCK

per together on the last evening that we were to pass on board of the *Ville de Saint Remy;* and while he did not make much of a reply to me he did mumble some sort of a purring answer that I took to mean he was willing, if I were, to make the trial.

Early that morning, while the rain still was falling, I had filled my two casks with fresh water; and after my breakfast I got them aboard the boat and then went to work at setting up my mast—using one of the davits in place of sheers and so managing the job very well. After that I had rigged the sail, and had set it to make sure that all was right; and then had furled it and lashed the boom fast on the roof of the cabin among the bags of coal—and with rather a heavy heart, too, for I knew that the chances were more than even against my ever getting to open water and fresh breezes, and so loosing again the knots which I had just tied. In the afternoon I had set my engine to going again for an hour, and then had banked my fires against the morning; and after that, until the shadows began to fall, I had spent my time in going over the list that I had made of my sea-stock to be sure that nothing that I needed was forgotten, and in taking a final general survey of my boat and its stores. And when darkness came the cat and I had our supper together—which was as good a one as the ship could provide us with—and when we had finished I told him, as I have said, what the chances were for and against our succeeding in our undertaking and in return asked him for an expression of his own views.

That he fully understood what I told him I am not prepared to say; but he certainly did answer me: jumping up on my lap and shoving his paws alternately against my stomach, and purring in so cheerful a fashion, and altogether making such a show of good spirits as to satisfy me that he was trying to tell me that we certainly would pull through. And my cat's promise of good luck fell in so exactly with my own confident hopes—which were rising strongly as the time for testing them got close at hand—that I hugged him tight to me very lovingly, and on my side promised that within another month or two he should stretch his legs in a mouse-hunt on dry land! And with that I put the lamp out and we turned in for the night.

XXXVII

HOW MY CAT STILL FARTHER CHEERED ME

It was in the grey of early morning, while the rain still was falling, that the cat and I had our breakfast; and as soon as the rain was over I was down in the boat, and had off the tarpaulin that covered her stern-sheets, and was busy bringing up my banked fires. One thing that I had learned how to do during the week that I had been testing my engine was to bank my fires well; and that was a matter of a good deal of importance to me—since every night during my voyage the fires would have to be kept that way, on the double score of my inability to hold my course in the darkness and of my need for sleep.

Presently I had steam up; and then I went back to the ship for the last and most important piece of cargo—my bag of jewels. It was with a queer feeling, half of doubt and half of exultation, that I fetched out this little bundle—still done up in the sleeve of the oilskin jacket—and stowed it in one of the lockers in the cabin of my boat. If my voyage went well, then all the rest of my life

—so far as wealth makes for happiness—would go well too: for in that rough and dirty little bag was such a treasure—that I had won away from the dead ship holding it—as would make me one of the richest men in the world. But against this exultant hope stood up a doubt so dark that there was no great room in my mind for cheerfulness: for as I stowed away the jewels in the boat I could not but think of those others who had stowed them away two hundred years and more before aboard the galleon; and who had started in their great ship well manned on a voyage in which the risk of disaster was as nothing in comparison with the risk that I had to face in the voyage that I was undertaking in my little boat alone. Yet their venture had ended miserably; and I, trying singly to accomplish what their whole company had failed in, very well might surrender the treasure again, as they had surrendered it, to the storm-power of the sea.

But thinking these dismal thoughts was no help to me, and so I choked them down and went once more aboard the steamer to make sure that I had forgotten nothing that I needed by taking a final look around. This being ended without my seeing anything that was necessary to me, I said good-bye to the *Ville de Saint Remy* and got down into my boat again; and my cat—who usually sat in the break of the side of the steamer while I was at

HOW MY CAT STILL CHEERED ME

work in the boat, though sometimes asking with a miau to be lifted down into her—of his own accord jumped aboard ahead of me: and that I took for a good sign.

Certainly, the cat and I made as queer a ship's company as ever went afloat together; and our little craft—with its cargo that would have bought a whole fleet's lading—was such an argosy as never before had sailed the seas. Nor did even Columbus, when he struck out across the black ocean westward, start upon a voyage so blind and so seemingly hopeless as was ours. The Admiral, at least, had with him such aids to navigation as his times afforded, and went cruising in open water; failing in his quest, the chance was free to him to put about again and so come once more to his home among living men. But I had not even his poor equipment; and as to turning again and so coming back to the point whence I started—even supposing that I could manage it—that ending to my voyage would be so miserable that it would be better for me to die by the way.

In none of the vessels through which I had searched had I found a sextant; nor would it have been of any use to me, had I found one, unless I had found also a chronometer still keeping time. Charts I did find; but as I had to know my position to get any good from them, and as I would run straight for any land that I sighted without in the least caring on what coast I made my landfall, I left them behind. My only aid to navigation was a compass, that I got from the binnacle of a ship lying near the *Ville de Saint Remy;* and aboard the same vessel I found a very good spyglass, and gladly brought it along with me because it would add to my chances—should I reach open water—not only of sighting a distant ship but of making out how she was standing in time to head her off.

But for all practical purposes the compass was enough for me. I knew that to the westward lay the American continent, and that between it and where I then was—for it was certain that I was not far south of the latitude of the Azores—was that section of the Atlantic which is more thickly crowded with ships than any other like-sized bit of ocean in the world. My chance of escape, therefore, and my only chance, lay in holding to a due west course: hoping first that, being clear of the weed, I might fall in with some passing vessel; and second that I might make the coast before a storm came on me by which my little boat would be swamped. And so I opened the throttle of my engine: and as the screw began to revolve I headed my boat for the cut in the weed which I had made when I was testing her—while my tow-rope drew taut and after me came slowly my long raft.

No doubt it was only because the hiss of the es-

HOW MY CAT STILL CHEERED ME

caping steam startled him; but at the first turn of the engine my cat scampered forward and seated himself in the very bows of the boat—a little black figure-head—and thence gazed out steadfastly westward as though he were the pilot charged with the duty of setting our vessel's course. He had to give place to me in a moment—when I went to the bows to begin my sawing through the weed—but I was cheered by his planting himself that way pointing our course with his nose for me: and again I took his bit of freakishness for a good sign.

XXXVIII

HOW I FOUGHT MY WAY THROUGH THE SARGASSO WEED

What I did on that first day of my voyage was what I did on every succeeding day during so long a time that it seemed to me the end of it never would come.

When my craft fairly was started, with the fire well fed and a light enough weight on the safety-valve to guard against any sudden chance rise in the steam pressure, I went forward to the bows with the compass and set myself to my sawing. The wheel being lashed with the rudder amidships, all the steering was managed from the bows—any deviation from the straight line westward being corrected by my taking the saw out from the guide-bars and cutting to the right or to the left with it until I had the boat's nose pointing again the right way. But there was not often need for cutting of this sort. Held by the guide-bars, the saw cut a straight path for the boat to follow; while, conversely, the boat held the saw true. And so, for the most part, I had only to stand like a machine there—endlessly hauling the saw up and endlessly thrusting it down. Behind me my little engine puffed and snorted; over the bows, below me, was the soft crunching sound of the weed opening as the boat thrust her nose into it; and on each side of me was the soft hissing rustling of the weed against the boat's sides. From time to time I would stop for sheer weariness—for anything more back-breaking than the steady working of that saw I never came across; and from time to time I had to stop my engine—which I managed, and also the starting of it, by means of a pair of lines brought forward into the bows from the lever-bar—while I attended to feeding the fire.

The only breaks in this deadly monotonous round were when I ate my meals—and at first these were as pleasant as they were restful, with the cat sitting beside me and eating very contentedly too—and when I fell in with a bit of wreckage that I had to steer clear of or to move out of my way. Interruptions of this latter sort — even though they gave me a change from my wearying sawing —were hard to put up with; for they not only held me back wofully, but they kept me in continual alarm lest I should break my saw. When the obstacle was a derelict, or anything so large that I could see it well ahead of me and so could have plenty of time in which to swing the boat to one side of it by slicing a diagonal way for her, I could get along without much difficulty; but when it was only a spar or a mast, so bedded in the weed that my first knowledge of it was finding it close under my bows, there was no chance to make a detour and I had to thrust it aside with a boat-hook or go to hacking at it with an axe until I had cut it through. And often it happened that I knew nothing at all of the obstacle, the weed covering it completely, until my saw struck against it; and that would send a cold shiver through me, as I whipped my saw out of the water—for I had only two saws with me, and I knew that to break one of them cut down my chances of escape by a half. Indeed, my first saw did get broken while I still was in the thick of the tangle; and after that I was in a constant tremor, which became almost agony when I felt the least jar in my cutting, for fear that the other would go too.

But with it all I managed to make pretty fair progress, and better than I had counted upon; for I succeeded in covering, as nearly as I could reckon it, close upon three miles a day. After I fairly got out upon my course I had no means whatever of judging distances; but my estimate of my advance was made at the end of my first day's run, when the wreck-pack still was in sight behind me and enabled me to make a close guess at how far I had come. As the sun went down that night over my bows — making a long path of crimson along the weed ahead of me, and filling the mist with a crimson glow — I still could make out, though very faintly, the continent of wrecks from which I had started; and with my glass I could distinguish the *Ville de Saint Remy* by the three flags which I had left flying on her masts. And the sight of her, and the thought of how comfortable and how safe I had been aboard of her, and of how I was done with her forever and was tying to as slim a chance of life as ever a man tied to, for a while put a great heaviness upon my heart. Not until darkness came and shut her out from me, and I was resting in my brightly lighted comfortable little cabin—with my supper to cheer me, and with my cat to cheer me too—did my spirits rise again; and I was glad, when I got under way once more in the morning, that the heavy mist cut her off from me—and that by the time the sun had thinned the mist a little I had made such progress as to put her out of sight of me for good and all.

Through my second day I still could make out the loom of the wreck-pack behind me — a dark line low down in the mist that I should have taken for a rain-cloud had I not known what it was; but that also was pretty well gone, by evening, and from my third day onward I was encompassed wholly by the soft veil of golden mist hanging low around me over the weed-covered sea. Only about noon time, when this veil grew thinner and had in it a brighter golden tone—or at sunset, when it was shot through with streams of crimson light which filled it with a ruddy glow—was it possible for me to see for more than a mile or so in any direction; and even when my horizon thus was enlarged a little my view still was the same: always the weed spread out over the water so thickly that nowhere was there the slightest break in it, and so dense and solid that it would have seemed like land around me but for its very gentle undulating motion—which made me giddy if I looked at it for long at a time. The only relief to this dull flat surface was when I came upon a wrecked ship, or upon a hummock of wreckage, rising a little up from it—also swaying very gently with a wearying motion that seemed as slow as time. And the silent despairing desolateness of it all sunk down into my very soul.

Even my cat seemed to feel the misery of that great loneliness and lost so much of his cheerfulness that he got to be but a dull companion for me; though likely enough what ailed him was the reflex of my own poor spirits, made low by my constant bodily weariness, and had I shown any liveliness he would have been lively too. But I was too tired to think much about him—or about anything else—as day after day I stood in the bow of the boat working my saw up and down with a deadly dull monotony: that had no break save when I stopped to rest a little my aching body, or to have a tussle with a bit of wreckage that barred my passage, or to stoke myself with food, or to put coal beneath my boiler, or to lie down at night with every one of my bones and muscles heavy with a dull pain.

And all the sound that there was in that still misty solitude was the puffing of my engine, and the wheel churning in the water, and the sharp hiss of the saw as it severed the matted fibres, and the crunching and rustling that the boat made as it went onward with a leaden slowness through the weed.

XXXIX

WHY MY CAT CALLED OUT TO ME

I HAD thought that I had struck the bed-rock of misery when I was wandering in the dead depths of the wreck-pack, with the conviction strong upon me that in a little while I would be dead there too. But as I look back upon that long suffering of lonely sorrow I think now that the worst of it came to me after I had left the wreck-pack behind. In that last round that I fought with misfortune the strength of my body was exhausted so completely that it could give no support to my spirit; and as the days went on and on—always with the same weed-covered sea around me and the same soft golden mist over me, and I always working wearily but with the stolid steadiness of a machine—so deadening a numbness took hold of me that I seemed to myself like some far-away strange person—yet one with whom I had a direct connection, and must needs sorrow for and sympathize with—struggling interminably through the dull jading mazes of a night-mare dream.

Once only was I aroused from this stupor of

WHY MY CAT CALLED OUT TO ME

spirit that went with my vigorous yet apathetic bodily action. Just at sunset one evening I sighted a vessel of some sort far ahead of me—a black mass looming uncertainly against the rich glow of crimson that filled the west—and for some reason or another I took into my head the fancy that I was nearing open water and that this was not a wreck but a living ship on board of which I would find living men: and at the thought of meeting with live men again I fairly cried with joy. Then darkness fell and shut her out from me; leaving me so eager that I could not sleep for thinking of her, and almost tempting me to press on through the night that I might be close up to her by dawn.

But when in the first faint grey light of early morning I made her out again, and saw that she was in just the same position and at just the same distance ahead of me, I was almost as sorry as I would have been had she vanished; for I knew that had she been a living ship in that long night-time she would have sailed away. And by noon, being then close upon her, I could see that she was floating bottom upwards: and so knew certainly that she was only a dead wreck drifting in slowly to take her place among the dead wrecks which I had left behind me; and beyond her, instead of open water, I saw only the weed-covered ocean stretching onward unbroken until it was lost in the golden haze.

IN THE SARGASSO SEA

Even then, though, I had a foolish hope that there might be living men clinging to her, and I edged my boat off its course a little so that I might run close under her stern. But no one showed on her hull as I neared her, and only my own voice broke the heavy silence as I crazily hailed her again and again. And then I fell into a dull rage with her, so weary was I of my loneliness and so bitter was my disappointment at finding her deserted—until suddenly a very different train of emotions was aroused in me as I made out slowly the weathered inverted lettering on her up-tilting stern, and so read her name there: *Golden Hind!*

Like a flash I had before me clearly all the details of my last moments aboard of her: my quick sharp words with Captain Luke, my step backward with my arms up as he and the mate pressed upon me, the smasher that I got in on the mate's jaw, the crack on my own head that stunned me—and then my revival of consciousness as I found myself adrift in the ocean and saw the brig sailing away. And while these thoughts crowded upon me my boat went onward through the weed slowly—and presently I had again parted company with the *Golden Hind*, and this time for good and all.

After that break in it my dull despairing weariness settled down upon me again—as the heavy days drifted past me and I pressed steadily on, and on, and on. How time went I do not know. I could keep no track of days which always were the same. But I must have been on my voyage for nearly a month when I fell in with the *Golden Hind:* as I know because a little while after passing her I used the last of the coal that was on the raft and cast it off—and my calculation at starting had been that the coal aboard the raft would last me for about thirty days.

Getting rid of the raft was a good thing for me in one way, for when the boat was relieved from that heavy mass dragging through the weed after her she went almost twice as fast. But in another way it was a bad thing for me, for it left me with only what coal I had on the boat herself—and, so far as I could judge from my surroundings, I was no nearer to being over the wall of my prison than I was on that first morning when I put off from the *Ville de Saint Remy.* Still the weed stretched away endlessly on all sides of me, and still the golden mist ceaselessly hung over me—only it did seem to me, though I did not trust myself to play much with this hopeful fancy, that the mist was a good deal thinner than it had been during the earlier part of my voyage.

But I was too broken to take much notice of my surroundings. Still I worked on and on, with the steadfastness and the hopelessness of a machine: up and down over the bows with my saw interminably, with only little breaks for rest and eating and to keep my fires up or for a struggle with a bit of wreckage that barred my way; and at night to weary sleep that did not rest me; and then up before sunrise to begin it all again with a fresh day that had no freshness in it—and was like all the many days of desperate toil which had gone before it, and like the others which still were to come.

Even when I saw ahead of me one morning a long lane of open water, a wide break in the weed, I was too dull to think much about it beyond steering my way into it thankfully—and then feeling a slow wonder as the boat slid along with no rustling noise on each side of her at what seemed to me an almost breathless speed. But as that day went on and the mist grew lighter and lighter about me and I came to more and more of these open spaces, and at the same time found that the weed between them was so much thinner that the boat almost could push through it without having a path cut for her, I began faintly to realize that perhaps I had got to the beginning of the end. And then, for the first time since I had lapsed into my stolid insensibility, a little weak thrill of hope went through me and I seemed to be waking from my despairing dream.

With the next day, however, hope full and strong fairly got hold of me: for I was out of the

WHY MY CAT CALLED OUT TO ME

mist completely, and the weed was so thin that I brought my saw inboard and finally had done with it, and the stretches of open water were so many and so large that I knew that the blessed free ocean must be very near at hand. And I think that my cat knew as well as I did that our troubles were close to a good ending; for all of a sudden he gave over his moping and fell to frisking about me and to going through all the tricks which I had taught him of his own accord; and thence onward he spent most of his time on the roof of the cabin—looking about him with a curious intentness, for all the world as though I had stationed him there to watch out for a ship bearing down on us, or for land. Even when I found that day that only a dozen bags of coal were left to me—for I had fed my furnace while my heaviness was upon me without paying any attention to how things were going with my stock of fuel—my spirits were none the worse for my discovery; for with every mile that I went onward the weed was growing thinner and I felt safe enough about continuing my voyage under sail.

Because my rousing out of my lethargy had been so slow, this change in my chances seemed to come upon me with a startling suddenness — when in reality, I suppose, I might have seen signs of it a good while sooner than I did see them had my mind been clear. But the actual end of my adventure, the resolving of my hopes into a glad certainty of rescue, really did come upon me with a rush at last.

We fairly were in open water, and the cat and I were dining in the cabin together very cheerfully—with the helm lashed and the boat going on her course at half speed. I was disposed to linger over my meal a little, for I was beginning to enjoy once more the luxury of getting rest when I rested, and when my cat suddenly left me and went on deck by himself—a thing that he never before had done—I took his desertion of me in ill part. A moment later I heard the padding of his feet on the roof of the cabin over me, and smiled to myself as I thought of him going on watch there; and then, presently, I heard him calling me—for I had come to understand a good many of his turns of language—with a lively "Miau!" But it was not until he called me again, and more urgently, that the oddness of his conduct came home to me and made me hurry on deck after him; and my first glance at him made me look in the direction in which he was looking eagerly: and there I saw the smoke of a steamer trailing black to the horizon, and beneath it her long black hull—and she was heading straight for me, and coming along at such a ripping rate that within twenty minutes she would be across my bows.

Half an hour more brought matters to a finish.

WHY MY CAT CALLED OUT TO ME

I had only to wait where I was until the steamer was close down upon me, and then to run in under her counter so that her people might throw me a line. Her whole side was crowded with faces as she stopped her way and I came up with her, and on her rail a tall officer was standing — holding fast with one hand to the rigging and having in the other a coil of rope all ready to cast.

One face among the many clustered there, and a mighty friendly one, was familiar to me; but I could not place it until a jolly voice hailed me that I recognized with a warm thrill — and the sound of it filled me with joy as I thought of my bag of jewels in the cabin locker, and of how at last my doctor's bill would be paid.

"And so it's yourself, my fine big young man, and at your old tricks again. But it's this time that you have the good luck of a black cat for company in your cruising all alone by yourself over the open sea!"

And then the tall officer with the coil of rope sung out "Catch!" — and sent the line whizzing down to me, and I caught the end of it in my hand.

THE END

By JAMES BARNES

A LOYAL TRAITOR. A Story of the War of 1812. Illustrated. Post 8vo, Cloth, Ornamental, $1 50.

A vigorous romance it is, full of life and adventure.—*N. Y. Herald.*

A stirring story. . . . The several characters are finely balanced and well drawn, and are admirably interwoven to give reasonableness and completeness in every chapter.—*Chicago Inter-Ocean.*

We turn with a feeling of relief to Mr. Barnes's breezy and Marryat-like story of the American privateersman. . . . This is all genuine romance, with a wide horizon and many changes of scene. . . . Mr. Barnes has done his work well.—*N. Y. Times.*

An excellent and intensely interesting story of romance and adventure.—*Brooklyn Standard-Union.*

The book has freshness, animation, and strong story-interest. —*Outlook, N. Y.*

A quick-moving, picturesque story. The daring Yankee sailor of that naval war, his life above deck and below, in battle and in cruise, his dialect and yarns, are all quaintly reproduced in a series of vivid scenes.—*Philadelphia Record.*

FOR KING OR COUNTRY. A Story of the American Revolution. Illustrated. Post 8vo, Cloth, Ornamental, $1 50.

NAVAL ACTIONS OF THE WAR OF 1812. Illustrated. 8vo, Cloth, Ornamental, $4 50.

NEW YORK AND LONDON
HARPER & BROTHERS, Publishers

☞ *The above works are for sale by all booksellers, or will be sent by mail by the publishers, postage prepaid, on receipt of the price.*

By ALBERT LEE

FOUR FOR A FORTUNE. A Tale. Illustrated by F. C. Yohn. Post 8vo, Cloth, Ornamental, $1 25.

The story is one of adventure and of treasure-hunting. A French sailor comes to New York having in his possession a half-burned chart, the writing on which he is unable to make out; he falls in with two Americans, to whom he shows his map, and they manage to locate the probable spot designated on the chart. The four start in search of the treasure, and have many thrilling and startling adventures both on land and on sea, the locality of the action being for the most part the picturesque little French colony of St. Pierre-Miquelon, off the south coast of Newfoundland.

TOMMY TODDLES. Illustrated by Peter Newell. 16mo, Cloth, $1 25.

There is plenty of droll fun in this book.... We pity the person who can refuse to grin at some of the jocund surprises, sprung like steel-traps by the story's comical turns, preposterous as it is.—*Independent,* N. Y.

TRACK ATHLETICS IN DETAIL. Compiled by the Editor of "Interscholastic Sport" in Harper's Round Table. Illustrated from Instantaneous Photographs. 8vo, Cloth, $1 25. (*In Harper's Round Table Library.*)

Of decided interest and just as decided value.—*Brooklyn Times.*

Indispensable to every aspirant for athletic honors.—*Philadelphia Bulletin.*

NEW YORK AND LONDON:
HARPER & BROTHERS, PUBLISHERS

SARGASSO SEA

THOMAS A JANVIER

www.ingramcontent.com/pod-product-compliance
Lightning Source LLC
Chambersburg PA
CBHW030747250426
43672CB00028B/1308